Optimal Performance Training for Football

Allen Hedrick

©2006 Coaches Choice. All rights reserved. Printed in the United States.

No part of this book may be reproduced, stored in a retrieval system, or transmitted, in any form or by any means, electronic, mechanical, photocopying, recording, or otherwise, without the prior permission of Coaches Choice. Throughout this book, the masculine shall be deemed to include the feminine and vice versa.

ISBN: 1-58518-958-8
Library of Congress Control Number: 2006928626
Book layout and cover design: Studio J Art & Design
Text photos: Barry Brown

Coaches Choice
P.O. Box 1828
Monterey, CA 93942
www.coacheschoice.com

Dedication

To my kids, Lindsey and Brandon—I am so glad I have had the experience of being your father. Thanks for making my life complete. To my wife Stephanie—you are the love of my life. I love all of you very much.

Acknowledgments

I would like to acknowledge a number of people who have played a significant role in my development as a strength and conditioning coach: Roberto Parker, who hired me as a graduate assistant at Fresno State and got me started in the profession; Steve Fleck, who gave me the wonderful opportunity to work at the Olympic Training Center in Colorado Springs; and Jack Braley, who gave me an even better opportunity by hiring me as his assistant at the Air Force Academy. Thank you all for giving me a chance. I also need to thank all of those coaches who I work with at the Academy. You make going to work a pleasure. Special thanks need to go to Coach Fisher DeBerry, who has enough confidence in me to allow me to go outside the box when designing the training programs for his athletes. I would be remiss if I didn't also thank all of the athletes who I have had the pleasure to work with at Fresno State, the Olympic Training Center, and the Air Force Academy. You are the best part of my job. Lastly, and most importantly, I thank God for blessing me and my family to the extent that He has. I am a very fortunate man.

I would be remiss if I did not give credit to Jeff Kipp, M.A., C.S.C.S., one of our assistant strength and conditioning coaches, for his assistance in the development of the speed, agility, and plyometric program presented in Chapter 4. We have integrated a lot of Jeff's ideas to enhance our training program.

contents

Dedication 3

Acknowledgments 4

Introduction 7

Chapter 1: Warming Up 9

Chapter 2: Flexibility 15

Chapter 3: Resistance Training 35

Chapter 4: Speed, Agility, and Plyometric Training 149

Chapter 5: Conditioning 177

About the Author 204

Optimal performance in football requires a total commitment to the strength and conditioning program. Winning starts with a complete dedication to the training program.

Introduction

The purpose of this book is to assist coaches in designing a training program, the goal of which is optimal performance in football. Football is a high-speed collision sport that demands a significant amount of time dedicated to training for top performance. Putting all the components together into a comprehensive training program can be a difficult task. Hopefully, with the help of the information presented here, that task will become less daunting.

However, I would like to make it clear right away that a "perfect training program" does not exist. Exercise physiology is not an exact science. Researchers are not at a point where they can say that there is one best way to train an athlete. Sometimes it seems that every study has another that contradicts its findings. What this means is that you often have to do some research and then make a decision about what direction you want to take with the design of your training program based on your educated guess and experience regarding what will work best for your athletes.

In addition, facility limitations may be an issue, either in the size of the training area or available equipment. These limitations may prevent you from including certain types of activities that you would like to provide to your athletes. Further, you are undoubtedly working with athletes with various levels of motivation, some of whom may not be as willing to adhere to the training protocol as you would like. All of these factors contribute to making your job of developing the most physically prepared team possible a challenging task.

It is not my goal for you to take the information provided in this book and apply it word for word. Each situation is unique, and you have your own ideas about what works best for your athletes. It therefore makes sense for you to apply those aspects of the information provided that best fit into your own situation and philosophy, with the goal of making your own training program the best it can be.

1

Warming Up

Warming up properly is necessary for optimal performance, both in training and competition.

Warming up and stretching are not the same thing. The goal during the warm-up is to raise the total body temperature to prepare the body for activity. During stretching, on the other hand, the goal is to increase range of motion. Most stretching techniques will not have a significant effect on body temperature. In fact, flexibility training should only occur after body temperature has been sufficiently increased.

The increase in body temperature that occurs during the warm-up is the result of three physiological processes that contribute to increased tissue temperature: the friction of the sliding filaments during muscular contraction, the metabolism of fuels, and the dilation of intramuscular blood vessels. But what are the benefits of increasing body temperature? The following physiologic changes occur during a warm-up and should have a positive effect on performance:

- An increase in muscular temperature results in the muscle contracting more forcefully and relaxing more quickly. As a result, speed and strength should be improved during exercise.
- The temperature of the blood traveling through the working muscles increases. As blood temperature rises, the amount of oxygen the blood can hold is reduced, which makes additional oxygen available to the working muscles.
- As the core temperature increases, the range of motion (ROM) around joints is enhanced.

The increase in ROM occurs because as core temperature increases, the viscosity of muscles, tendons, and ligaments is reduced. Therefore, many researchers believe that stretching should be done only after a proper warm-up. The physiological responses that occur during the warm-up justify it as a method to prepare the body for flexibility training.

Unfortunately, the prepractice and precompetition warm-up program used by many teams often consists chiefly of static stretching. However, using static stretching in an attempt to increase core temperature has three major disadvantages.

- Minimal friction of the sliding filaments occurs because of the passive nature of static stretching.
- Little, if any, increase occurs in the rate of fuels being metabolized.
- Intramuscular blood vessels do not dilate in response to static stretching.

These disadvantages, combined with the minimal elevation in core body temperature that occurs during static stretching, show why static stretching is an ineffective warm-up technique. As a result, athletes using static stretching to warm up are missing out on the benefits that should be taking place during that portion of the workout—decreased viscosity of muscle and reduced stiffness in the muscles and joints.

Warming up should be the foundation of a successful practice or training session. Properly warming up is the key to being able to achieve the intensity necessary to realize optimal results. Regrettably, many athletes elect to take short cuts during the warm-up process, leading to poor performance during a workout or competition.

Types of Warm-up

Three main types of warm-up are available: passive, general, and specific. Regardless of which method is adopted, the primary purpose of warming up prior to physical activity should be to elevate muscle temperature. In reality, differences exist among the various options concerning the degree to which this objective is met.

Passive

A passive warm-up utilizes methods such as hot showers, heating pads, and massage (Figure 1-1). Research has generally shown that passive warm-up methods do not result in the desired increases in tissue temperature.

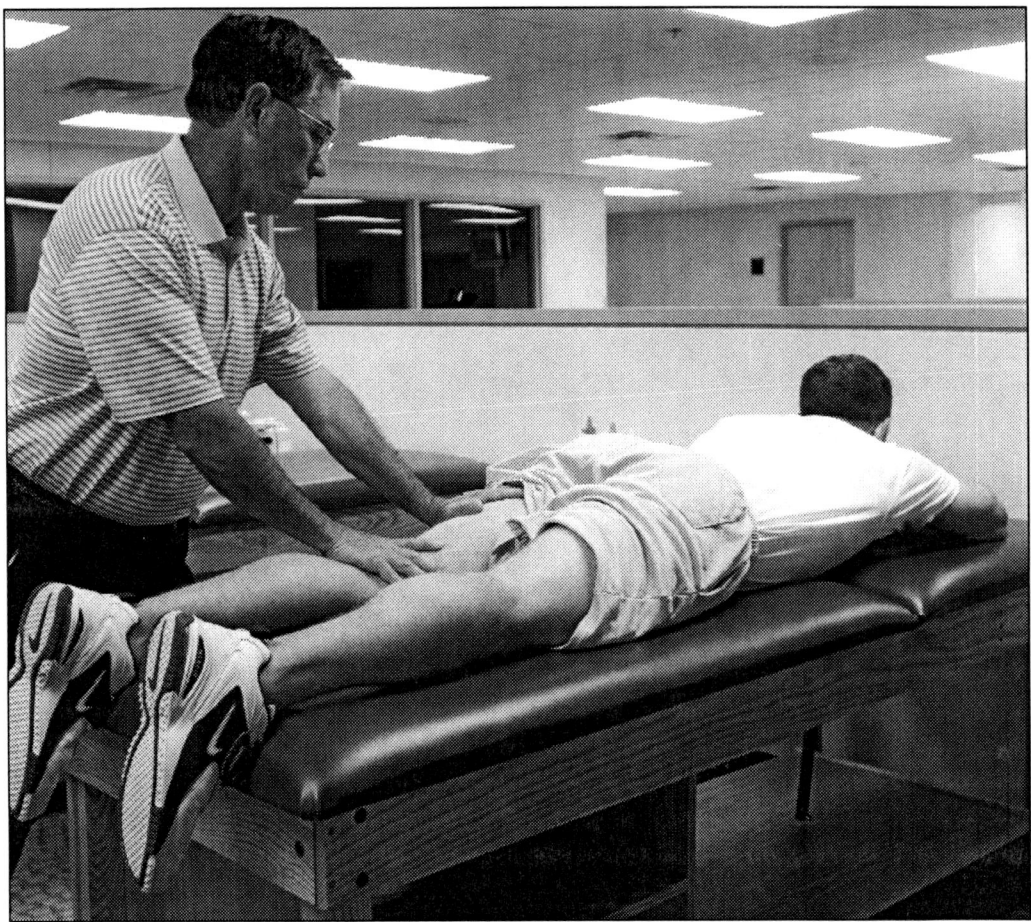

Figure 1-1. Passive warm-up methods include hot showers, heating pads, and massage.

General

General warm-ups involve fundamental activities that require movement of the major muscle groups, such as jogging, cycling, or jumping rope (Figure 1-2). Because the major muscle groups are recruited in these types of activities, a general warm-up is more effective at increasing tissue temperature than a passive warm-up, and is more appropriate when preparing the body for demanding physical activity.

Figure 1-2. General warm-up activities include jogging, cycling, or jumping rope.

Specific

A specific warm-up involves movements that are specific to the sport activity, such as a baseball player taking batting practice or a quarterback throwing passes during pregame warm-ups. The advantage of a specific warm-up is that not only does an increase in tissue temperature occur, but also rehearsal of the specific movements of the activity about to take place (Figure 1-3). This specificity provides the additional benefit of improving the neural responses required during the activity.

Warm-up Guidelines

The number of repetitions, the intensity, and the duration must be considered when designing the warm-up session. The length of the warm-up period will depend on both the climate and the athlete's physical conditioning level. A general guideline is that the warm-up activity should last approximately five to 15 minutes and be long enough for the individual to break out in a sweat.

In terms of the climate, the higher the outside or room temperature, the shorter the warm-up. Again, sweat can be used as an indicator of the effectiveness of the warm-up

Figure 1-3. Specific warm-up activities are specific to the activity that is about to be performed, such as a quarterback throwing passes during pre-game warm-ups, or an athlete performing gradually higher intensity cleans as a way to warm up for a workout.

period. In contrast to what many athletes assume, as the conditioning level of the athlete improves, the intensity and duration of the warm-up should increase. Explain to your athletes that as they become better conditioned, the thermoregulatory system is better able to respond to the heat produced during exercise. As a result, a well-conditioned individual will likely require a longer and/or more intense warm-up to achieve the desired increase in body temperature as compared to a less-conditioned individual.

A Practical Example

A variety of techniques can be used to achieve the goal of increasing core temperature, such as stationary cycling, jumping rope, and jogging. However, limitations exist when using these types of activities to warm up. First of all, when working in a group setting, using equipment such as stationary cycles or stairclimbers means that you need to have enough equipment available for everyone in the group, which may be impractical in terms of both space and cost. Jump ropes are obviously less expensive and require less room to store, but they provide some limitations in terms of the variety of movements that can be performed.

It is more effective, in terms of space, cost, and variety of movement, to have the athletes form a single-file line and jog around the weight room while playing a simple game of follow the leader. The leader performs a variety of movements while jogging around the room, such as running backwards, weaving in, around, and over equipment, sliding laterally, skipping, and so on. The variety of movements that can be performed is limited only by the creativity of the leader. Using this process requires no equipment and is very effective at increasing core temperature because of the variety of large muscle groups that can be involved. As previously suggested, the warm-up activity should be performed at a duration and intensity that causes the athletes to begin sweating by the end of the warm-up session.

For lower-intensity, less-complex activities (such as jogging), this general warm-up session will be sufficient to prepare the athlete to participate. For higher-intensity, more-complex activities (such as weightlifting, plyometrics, or speed training) this general warm-up activity should be followed by a specific warm-up. For example, if an athlete was going to perform cleans to start his workout, he could start with the general warm-up just described, then continue the warm-up process by performing two to four low-intensity cleans and gradually increasing the intensity of the activity until reaching a weight just below the training weight to be lifted on the first work set. The actual number of warm-up sets needed depends primarily on the required intensity of the first set. The higher the intensity, the greater the number of warm-up sets required.

2

Flexibility

A well-designed flexibility-training program is an important part of the overall strength and conditioning program.

Flexibility is an important component of any training program. Achieving an adequate level of flexibility helps eliminate inefficient movement by allowing the joints to move freely through their full, normal ranges of motion (ROM). Enhancing flexibility may also reduce the incidence of muscle injury.

Flexibility also has a positive effect on the performance of various movement skills. However, it is important to note that, while some great athletes are very flexible, this high level of flexibility is not what makes them great athletes. The purpose of flexibility training is not to achieve an extraordinary level of flexibility, but instead to achieve a level of flexibility that can allow the athlete to move effectively.

Flexibility training plays an important role in injury prevention. One of the more frequent problems seen in athletes with poor flexibility is lower-back pain, potentially resulting from tight quadriceps, iliopsoas, and back muscles (with perhaps a corresponding weakness in the abdominals and hamstrings). A lack of adequate flexibility can also increase the incidence of muscle tears resulting from tight muscles on one or both sides of a joint. A good rule to follow regarding the relationship between flexibility and injury is that a normal ROM is needed in each joint to protect against injury. If an athlete is involved in a sport that requires greater than normal ROM, then a higher level of flexibility will be needed to protect against injury.

Because of the important benefits that flexibility provides, you should supervise flexibility training just like you would any other part of the training session. Doing so emphasizes the importance of flexibility training and may encourage athletes to keep their attention focused on the task at hand.

Types of Flexibility Training

Numerous stretching methods are used to enhance flexibility. The most common flexibility-training methods are static, ballistic, and various proprioceptive neuromuscular facilitation (PNF) techniques. Although not as common as the three methods just mentioned, dynamic flexibility is also gaining acceptance.

Methods of flexibility training can also be categorized as either active or passive. An active stretch occurs when the person stretching provides the force necessary to perform the stretch. For example, when performing a sitting toe touch, the athlete provides the force required to lean forward and stretch the hamstrings and lower back. In contrast, an example of a passive stretch might involve a situation in which a partner or stretching device pushes or pulls on the athlete, thereby causing the stretch to occur.

Whichever flexibility-training method is used, the critical factor is that the exercises are performed correctly. Performing any stretch with incorrect technique is at best going to reduce the effectiveness of the training and at worst increase the risk for injury. Stated simply, stretches must be performed with good technique if optimal increases in flexibility are to occur.

Static Stretching

The most commonly used method to increase flexibility is static stretching (Figure 2-1). A slow, constant speed is used during this type of stretch, with the final position held for approximately 30 seconds. Static stretching involves the relaxation and simultaneous lengthening of the stretched muscle. Because static stretching is performed slowly, it does not activate the stretch reflex, thereby reducing the risk of injury. While injury to muscles or connective tissue can still result if the intensity of the static stretch is too great, no drawbacks are associated with static stretching with regards to injury potential, as long as proper techniques are used. However, it is important to note that research suggests that using static flexibility prior to taking part in dynamic activities (e.g., running, jumping, and throwing) can actually have a negative effect on performance.

Figure 2-1. Static flexibility involves slowly moving into the stretched position and then holding that stretch for 30 seconds.

No advantage has been found in increasing the length of time the stretched position is held. Increasing the duration of the stretch to 60 seconds does not improve flexibility any more than holding a stretch for 30 seconds. Reaching the final static stretch position should be done slowly and only to a point of minor discomfort. The amount of tension should diminish as the stretch is held. If a reduction in tension does not occur, the stretched position should be reduced slightly. Using this technique will likely avoid activation of the stretch reflex.

Static stretching performed correctly will result in little or no soreness, and minimal energy is required. Athletes should adhere to the following protocol for static stretching:
- Perform a five- to 10-minute warm-up, with a duration and intensity that causes them to begin to sweat.
- Emphasize slow, smooth movements. They should hold the stretch for 30 seconds as they breathe normally, and then exhale as they slowly stretch

further, to a point just short of discomfort. They then hold for 30 seconds again. Athletes should repeat the stretch three times and focus on staying relaxed.
- Slightly reduce the ROM of any stretch that hurts, because they are stretching too far.
- Stretch only to their limits.
- Avoid locking their joints.
- Avoid bouncing, which will reduce the possibility of stimulating the muscle spindles.
- Stretch large muscle groups first and repeat the same routine every time they stretch.
- Be consistent with the time of day they do their stretches, remembering that they are least flexible in the morning.
- Stretch again after exercise, when the core temperature is optimally elevated (for optimal increases in flexibility).

Ballistic Stretching

Ballistic stretching can be thought of as a rapid, jerky, uncontrolled movement in which the body part is put into motion and momentum carries it through the ROM until the muscles are stretched to their limits (Figure 2-2). A negative aspect of ballistic stretching is that the increase in ROM occurs through a series of jerks or pulls on the tissue. Because ballistic stretching occurs at high speeds, trying to control the rate and degree of stretch and the force applied to induce the stretch is difficult. In addition, ballistic stretching may injure muscles or connective tissues, especially when an injury has previously taken place. This increase in injury rate occurs because of the danger of exceeding the extensibility limits of the tissue being stretched.

Figure 2-2. Ballistic flexibility involves rapid, jerky, uncontrolled movements that may lead to injury.

Ballistic stretching is no longer considered an appropriate method for increasing ROM. When comparing static- and ballistic-stretching techniques, four distinct disadvantages of ballistic stretching stand out:
- Increased danger of exceeding the limits of the tissues involved
- Higher energy requirements
- Increased incidence of muscular soreness
- Activation of the stretch reflex

Muscle spindles and Golgi tendon organs are sensory organs in skeletal muscle that act as protective mechanisms against injury during passive and active stretching. Muscle spindles are located within the center of a muscle. When muscle spindles are stimulated, the muscle contracts, thereby hindering increases in flexibility. When this internal tension develops in the muscle, the muscular contraction prevents it from being fully stretched. A typical example of this reflex is the knee-jerk response. When the patellar tendon is struck, the tendon, and consequently the quadriceps muscle, experiences a slight, but rapid, stretch. The induced stretch activates the muscle spindle receptors within the quadriceps.

During rapid stretching activity, a sensory neuron from the muscle spindle innervates a motor neuron in the spine. The motor neuron then causes a muscle action of the previously stretched extramural muscle fibers—this action is the stretch reflex. Because ROM is limited by the reflexive muscle action, stimulation of the muscle spindle and the subsequent activation of the stretch reflex should be avoided during stretching.

The other sensory organ is the Golgi tendon organ, which is located at the musculotendinous junction. When excessive force is generated in the muscle, the Golgi tendon organ causes a reflex opposite that of the muscle spindle by inhibiting muscle contraction and causing the muscle to relax. The Golgi tendon organ helps prevent injury by preventing the muscle from developing too much force or tension during active stretching.

Proprioceptive Neuromuscular Facilitation

Proprioceptive neuromuscular facilitation (PNF) was originally developed as part of an approach that was designed to relax muscles. Its use has since expanded to the conditioning programs of athletes as a way to increase musculoskeletal flexibility (Figure 2-3). Over the years, PNF has become widely accepted as a successful method of increasing ROM.

PNF techniques are generally performed with a partner and make use of both passive movement and active (concentric and isometric) muscle actions. While various PNF methods exist, the most commonly used technique involves slowly placing the muscle/joint in a static-stretch position while keeping the muscle relaxed. After holding the stretched position for about 20 seconds, the muscle is contracted for 10 seconds with a strong isometric contraction against external force acting in the direction of the stretch. The external force should be sufficient to prevent any movement in the joint. Then, the muscle/joint is briefly taken out of the stretched position and a second

Figure 2-3. Proprioceptive neuromuscular facilitation (PNF) stretching makes use of a partner and typically involves alternating between contracting and relaxing the muscle tissue surrounding the joint(s) being stretched.

stretch is performed, potentially resulting in a greater stretch. The isometric contraction that is used in PNF stretching stimulates the respective Golgi tendon organs, helping to maintain low muscle tension during the terminal stretching maneuver. This low muscle tension allows the connective tissues to stretch through a greater ROM, thereby increasing flexibility.

Some studies suggest that PNF produces larger increases in ROM than does static stretching. However, the required techniques can be impractical to use. One of the limitations of using PNF is that a partner is often required, meaning that only half the team is stretching at any given time. Further, the partner has to be very careful to not overstretch the muscle, making the technique potentially dangerous unless each person is familiar with the correct techniques. In fact, many organizations in the fitness industry strongly recommend that their certified personal trainers not lead this type of stretching without adequate training. For this reason, and because the research advocating the effectiveness of PNF has been disputed in some subsequent studies, this technique is not recommended in this setting.

Dynamic Stretching

Although dynamic flexibility is not a new technique, it is not as commonly used as the other flexibility-training methods (Figure 2-4). While dynamic stretching is similar to ballistic stretching in that it utilizes speed of movement, dynamic stretching avoids bouncing and includes movements specific to a sport or movement pattern.

Some debate is ongoing regarding dynamic flexibility. But, if you accept the specificity of training principle and apply that principle to flexibility, it should eliminate that controversy. Flexibility is frequently measured statically by tests such as the sit-and-

Figure 2-4. Dynamic flexibility consists of functional-based movements and better adheres to the concept of flexibility than do other types of flexibility training.

reach test. Unfortunately, research has shown that no correlation exists between static flexibility and dynamic performance. Few instances will arise in which the ability to achieve a high degree of static flexibility is advantageous. Although dynamic-flexibility training is not as commonly used as the other flexibility methods previously discussed, some unique aspects of dynamic flexibility may warrant its use. Applying the principle of specificity, dynamic flexibility is more applicable to athletic performance because it more closely duplicates normal movement patterns.

Research needs to continue before definitive answers regarding flexibility training can be provided. However, it can be said that coaches need to evaluate the flexibility-training techniques they utilize and question why they do so. Specifically, using static stretching as part of a warm-up is common. However, the research—and logic—makes it clear that static stretches will do little to prevent injuries or improve muscle function prior to activity. Dynamic-flexibility movements, on the other hand, when taken through the full ROM, and started slowly before building up to movement-specific speeds, are more appropriate, both preexercise and in the development of active ROM for sports performance.

Dynamic stretching consists of functional-based exercises. As training progresses, dynamic-stretching exercises can be made more effective by progressing, for example, from a standing position to a walk, and then to a skip or run. Replacing static-stretching exercises with dynamic ones is not difficult. Many times, the actual stretching exercise is the same, but it is preceded and followed by some form of movement.

Individuals wishing to implement dynamic-flexibility programs should begin dynamic stretches with low-volume, low-intensity training. Dynamic-flexibility exercises require balance and coordination, and a short period of time exists after dynamic-flexibility training is introduced during which muscle soreness may occur.

Factors Affecting Flexibility

A number of factors influence flexibility. Some of these factors (e.g., joint structure, age, gender) cannot be altered by training. However, other factors (e.g., core temperature, muscle and connective-tissue pliability, activity level, hyperlaxity) can be influenced by training.

Joint Structure

The structure of the joint is one of the primary limiting factors in determining ROM, in that joint structure defines a clear limit to how much movement is available. Joint structures vary from individual to individual, and must be considered when evaluating flexibility.

Flexibility is highly specific to the joint being assessed (Figure 2-5). It is not unusual for an individual to be very flexible in one joint and have limited flexibility in another. In other words, flexibility is not a general characteristic, but instead is specific to each particular joint and joint action. Therefore, performing a single flexibility test to measure overall flexibility is a mistake.

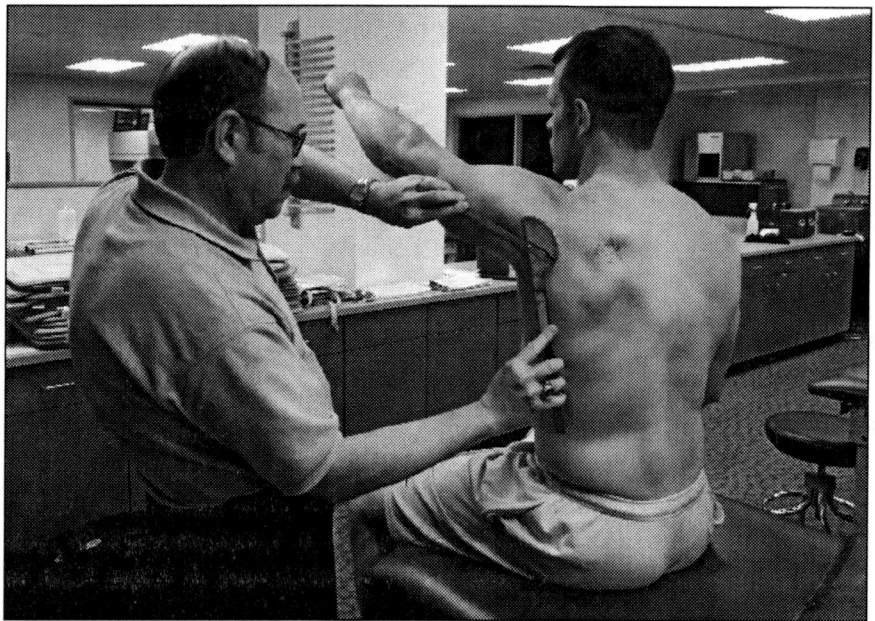

Figure 2-5. Static flexibility can be assessed with the use of a goniometer.

Age

Age is also a consideration in flexibility. It has been found that flexibility decreases in elementary school children, reaching a low point between 10 and 12 years of age. Flexibility usually improves from this point, but never to the extent found during early childhood. This loss in flexibility is the result of a gradual loss of elasticity in the muscles.

Childhood is the optimal time to begin flexibility training. Young athletes have a high level of flexibility, so prepubescence represents the optimal stage for starting to work on flexibility. Training programs should be aimed at developing flexibility in all joints during this stage.

Gender

Females are generally more flexible than males. Elementary school girls are more flexible than boys, and this difference likely exists throughout adult life. This higher degree of flexibility in females is due to anatomical variations in joint structures. The biggest differences in flexibility are seen in the trunk (flexion and extension), hips, and ankles. The decrease in flexibility seen in boys at puberty is thought to be related to increases in muscle size, stature, and muscle strength. Gender does not seem to be a factor in flexibility during prepubescence. If gender plays any role in flexibility during prepubescence, its effects are not evident until just prior to the onset of puberty.

Core Temperature

Range of motion is positively affected by an increase in either core temperature or external temperature. Because of the positive effect that increasing core temperature has on ROM, it is critical that you emphasize the importance of warming up prior to participating in flexibility training.

Muscle and Connective Tissue

Connective tissue (i.e., the ligaments and tendons) is the most important target of ROM exercises. Although muscle itself is not considered a connective-tissue structure, evidence suggests that when a relaxed muscle is stretched, perhaps all of the resistance to the stretch is derived from the extensive connective-tissue framework and sheathing within and around the muscle. In normal circumstances, connective tissue is the major structure limiting joint ROM. Thus, improvements in ROM as a result of stretching are primarily due to connective-tissue adaptations.

Most of the variation between individuals in ROM is the result of the elastic properties of the muscle and tendons attached across the joints. "Stiff" muscles and tendons reduce ROM while "compliant" muscles and tendons increase ROM. The elastic properties are altered as a result of stretching exercises.

Joint structure varies from joint to joint. As a result of their structure, some joints offer a reduced range of movement when compared to other joints. For example, hinge joints like the knee and elbow allow only backward and forward movement (flexion and extension). In contrast, the ball-and-socket joints of the hip and shoulder allow movements in all anatomical planes and have the greatest ROM of all joints.

The muscles crossing over, or adjacent to, a joint will also affect flexibility at that joint. During movement, the active contraction of the acting, or agonist, muscle is synchronized with the relaxation or stretching of the antagonistic muscle. The more effectively the antagonistic muscles yield, the less energy is required to overcome their resistance. The ability of a muscle fiber to lengthen increases as a result of flexibility training. If the antagonistic muscles are not relaxed, or if a lack of coordination exists between contraction (agonists) and relaxation (antagonists), increases in flexibility will be hindered.

Activity Level

Physically active individuals are generally more flexible than their inactive counterparts, because connective tissues tend to become less pliable when exposed only to the limited ranges of motion common in people with sedentary lifestyles (Figure 2-6). A decrease in activity level will also result in an increase in percent body fat and a decrease in the pliability of connective tissue. In addition, an increase in fat deposits around the joints creates obstructions to range of motion.

Figure 2-6. Physical activity plays a role in flexibility, as physically active people tend to be more flexible than those who are more sedentary.

One type of activity that can have an impact on an individual's flexibility level is resistance training. On one hand, a well-designed and properly executed resistance-training program can increase flexibility. On the other hand, heavy resistance training performed through a limited range of motion may decrease flexibility. To avoid decreases in ROM, resistance-training programs should be designed to develop both agonist and antagonist muscles. Furthermore, exercises should be executed through the full available ROM of the involved joints.

While improper strength training can negatively affect ROM, this result is normally not due to the person becoming too muscular. Instead, the decrease in flexibility occurs because of the improper development of a muscle or muscle group around a joint, resulting in a restriction of motion at that joint. For example, a person with large biceps and deltoids may experience difficulty in stretching the triceps, racking a power clean, or holding a bar while performing the front squat.

Hyperlaxity

Although not common, some individuals are born with a tissue structure that predisposes them to hyperlaxity, which allows the joints of the body to achieve an unusually wide range of motion. These individuals must take caution when implementing a stretching program. It is important to avoid overstretching and creating even greater levels of laxity in the surrounding supportive tissues. Problems can arise when individuals with hyperlaxity are placed in a stretching program without being properly assessed by a healthcare professional. Poor selection of stretching exercises can cause problems for these athletes.

Flexibility-Training Adaptations

Flexibility training results in two different tissue adaptations: elastic and plastic. Elasticity is the ability to return to the original resting length after a passive stretch, which results in a *temporary* change in length. Contrast that with plasticity, which is the tendency to assume a new and greater length after a passive stretch, even after the load is removed, meaning that a *permanent* change in length results.

Muscle has elastic properties only. Ligaments and tendons, in contrast, have both plastic and elastic properties. When connective tissue is stretched, some of the elongation occurs in the elastic tissue elements and some occurs in the plastic elements. When the stretch is removed, the elastic deformation recovers, but the plastic deformation remains.

Clearly, stretching techniques should be designed to result in a plastic deformation, because permanently increasing ROM is the goal of flexibility training. During stretching, the proportion of elastic and plastic deformation varies, depending on how and under what conditions the flexibility training occurs. Emphasize stretching to the point of mild discomfort, and encourage your athletes to hold the stretched position for an extended period of time and stretch only after core temperature has been elevated. These techniques will maximize the plastic properties of a stretch.

Recommended Flexibility Routine and Guidelines

A combination of dynamic and static flexibility training is recommended when the program goal is increased range of motion. The more functional the training, the more benefit it provides to those taking part in the training program. Dynamic flexibility alone can be limiting because some joints and muscle groups (e.g., neck, shoulders) may be more effectively stretched using static-stretching techniques.

Dynamic-Flexibility Guidelines

Share the following recommendations with your athletes when you are implementing a dynamic-flexibility training program:
- Do not overemphasize flexibility; use moderation and common sense.
- If it hurts, the athlete should not do it. No one should force any stretch.

- Strength training should be combined with flexibility training.
- The development of flexibility should be joint-specific.
- Orient the athlete's body in the most functional position relative to the joint or muscle to be stretched and relative to the particular activity in which the athlete is engaged.
- Develop a flexibility routine specific to the demands of the sport and the qualities of the individual athlete.
- Improvements in flexibility can occur day to day. After ROM is increased or developed to the desired level, it is easy to maintain that degree of flexibility. Less time and effort is needed to maintain flexibility than to improve it.
- Athletes should try to stretch large muscle groups first.
- Athletes should stretch regularly. Remind your players that flexibility is hindered in the morning.
- The best time to stretch to optimally increase ROM is after exercise, when core temperature is maximally elevated. Think in terms of stretching prior to training or competition to help prevent injury and stretching after a workout or competition to optimally increase range of motion.

Unfortunately, little published information provides guidelines specific to dynamic-flexibility training. It would seem that much of the protocol provided for static-flexibility training could be applied to dynamic-flexibility training programs as well. Most importantly, a warm-up period should occur before any flexibility training. Training frequency should be two to five times per week, depending on the flexibility level of the athlete. Because dynamic flexibility is performed during movement, each stretch should be repeated over a distance of 20 to 25 yards.

When an Athlete Should Stretch and Why

As already mentioned, a warm-up session should precede each training session. After the core temperature has been elevated, it may be necessary to immediately conduct flexibility training, depending on the intensity of the activity to follow. For example, if the athlete is going to participate in sprint training following the warm-up, stretching prior to activity would be necessary. However, if the athlete was going to go jogging, flexibility training could wait until after the training session was complete.

Dynamic-Stretching Exercise Techniques

The following is a list of dynamic-flexibility exercises, along with a description of each. The exercises presented are based on movements that occur in the game of football. As a result, this is not an all-inclusive list of dynamic stretches, which would be limited only by your creativity when designing the flexibility-training program. All exercises described here are performed while walking over a distance of 20 to 25 yards.

The frequency with which flexibility training occurs depends both on the flexibility requirements of the sport and the exercise/training habits of the individual athlete. If an athlete has a lack of flexibility that is hindering performance, then flexibility training should take place three to five times per week. If an athlete already has adequate flexibility and the goal is to maintain his level of flexibility, then the frequency of training can be reduced to as little as two times per week.

Likewise, if an athlete participates in explosive or high-speed activities such as weightlifting or sprinting, then flexibility training will naturally occur more frequently because of the need to stretch prior to these types of activities. However, if the athlete participates in slower, more controlled activities such as riding a stationary bike or performing circuit training, the need for frequent stretching is reduced.

Arm Circles (Figure 2-7)

- While walking over the prescribed distance, the athlete alternates performing arm circles with the right and left arms.
- The athlete performs arm circles with the arm straight, progressing from having the arm hanging at his side to a position where his arm is directly overhead.
- He must perform these circles in both a forward and backward motion over a full, comfortable ROM.

Arm Swings (Figure 2-8)

- While slowly walking over the prescribed distance, the athlete keeps the arms straight and lifts them to shoulder height, alternately performing arm swings with the right and left arms.
- He should keep the hand pointed directly lateral to the shoulder.
- While keeping the arm straight and at shoulder height, the athlete should first swing the arm across the chest and then as far back as possible through a full, comfortable ROM.
- Remind the exercisers to alternate arms with each step.

Figure 2-7. Arm circles

Figure 2-8. Arm swings

Figure 2-8. Arm swings

27

Lunge Walk (Figure 2-9)

- The athlete begins by clasping his hands behind his head.
- He steps forward and drops into a lunge position. He must not allow the knee of the forward leg to move beyond the toes. The back knee should be just off the floor. Remind the exerciser to keep his head up and his back arched with the torso leaning back slightly.
- He should pause for a count in the bottom position and then repeat with the opposite leg, progressing forward with each step.

Lunge Walk/Palms to Floor (Figure 2-10)

- With his hands at his sides, the athlete steps forward and drops into a lunge position.
- He must not allow the knee of the forward leg to move beyond his toes. The back knee should be just off the floor. At the bottom position, he places each palm on the floor with the fingers pointing forward.
- He should pause for a count in the bottom position and then repeat with the opposite leg, progressing forward with each step.

Figure 2-9. Lunge walk

Figure 2-10. Lunge walk/palms to floor

Twisting Lunge Walk (Figure 2-11)

- The athlete begins by clasping his hands behind his head.
- He then steps forward and drops into a lunge position. As he does so, he twists the upper body so that the left elbow touches the outside of the right (forward) leg. He should pause in that position for a count, and then twist so that the right elbow touches the inside of the right leg.
- He must not allow the knee of the forward leg to move beyond the toes. The back knee should be just off the floor. He should keep his head up and his back arched with the torso leaning back slightly.
- He then repeats the exercise with the left leg, touching the outside of the leg with the right elbow and the inside with the left elbow, progressing forward with each step.

Hockey Lunge Walk (Figure 2-12)

- The athlete begins by clasping his hands behind his head.
- He then steps forward, placing the front foot eight to 10 inches outside the shoulder, and drops into a lunge position. He must keep the feet pointing directly forward and must not allow the knee of the forward leg to move beyond the toes. The back knee should be just off the floor. He should keep his head up and his back arched with the torso leaning back slightly.
- He should pause for a count in the bottom position and then repeat with the opposite leg, progressing forward with each step.

Figure 2-11. Twisting lunge walk

Figure 2-12. Hockey lunge walk

Reverse Lunge Walk (Figure 2-13)

- The athlete begins by clasping his hands behind his head.
- He then steps backward and drops into a lunge position. He must not allow the knee of the forward leg to move beyond the toes. The back knee should be just off the floor. He should keep his head up and his back arched with the torso leaning back slightly.
- He should pause for a count in the bottom position and then repeat with the opposite leg, progressing backward with each step.

Walking Side Lunge (Figure 2-14)

- The athlete begins by turning sideways, with the right shoulder pointing in the direction he is going.
- He then takes a long lateral step with the right foot. Keeping the left leg straight, he sinks the hips back and to the right. He must not allow the right knee to move beyond the toes of the right foot. He should keep the back arched.
- He should pause for a count at the bottom, stand up, pivot, and then repeat the movement with the left leg leading.

Figure 2-13. Reverse lunge walk   Figure 2-14. Walking side lunge

Lunge Out on All Fours/Walk Hands Between (Figure 2-15)

- The athlete begins by lunging out on all fours, with his body extended out and supported on the hands and feet.
- Keeping the hands stationary, he walks the feet up between his hands. He must keep the legs straight.
- At the top of the movement, he lunges out on all fours again and repeats the movement. He must attempt to get the feet slightly further through the hands with each repetition.

Walking Knee Tuck (Figure 2-16)

- The athlete steps forward with the left leg and, using both hands to assist the movement, pulls his right knee up to his chest.
- He then pauses for a count, steps with the right leg, and repeats the action with the left leg. He must try to pull the knee slightly higher with each repetition.

Figure 2-15. Lunge out on all fours/walk hands between

Figure 2-16. Walking knee tuck

Figure 2-17. Walking knee over hurdles

Walking Knee Over Hurdles (Figure 2-17)

- The athlete must imagine a line of intermediate hurdles lined up along a track, alternating to the right and left sides of his body.
- He leads with the right knee and lifts the right leg up and over the first hurdle. He then places the right foot down and repeats the movement with the left leg. He must attempt to get each leg slightly higher over the hurdle with each repetition.

Walking Knee Tuck/Lift the Foot (Figure 2-18)

- The athlete begins by stepping forward with the left leg and, using both hands to assist the movement, squeezes the right knee up to the chest and then pauses for a count.
- While in this position, he moves his right hand to his right foot and pulls his leg back and up, trying to pull the foot to shoulder height behind him while standing tall.
- He pauses for a count, then steps with the right leg and repeats the action with the left leg.

Figure 2-18. Walking knee tuck/lift the foot

Head Circles (Figure 2-19)

- From a standing position, the athlete slowly begins moving his head in a circle. As the movement becomes more comfortable, he should try to increase the size of the circle.
- He then repeats the movement in the opposite direction.

Head Front to Back (Figure 2-20)

- From a standing position, the athlete slowly begins moving his head front to back. As the movement becomes more comfortable, he should try to increase the range of motion of the movement, slowly tilting the head further forward and further back.

Figure 2-19. Head circles

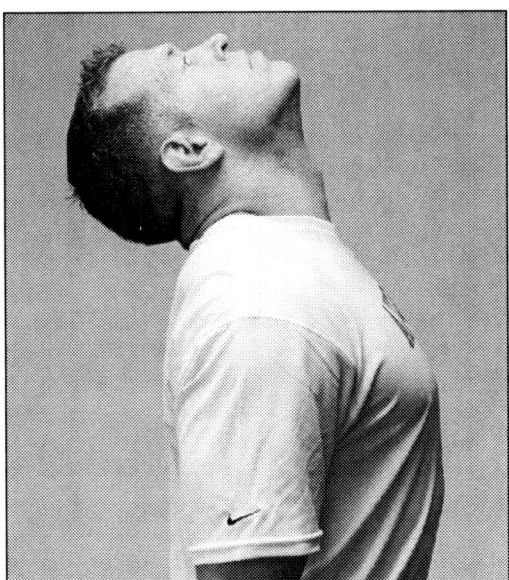

Figure 2-20. Head front to back

Head Side to Side (Figure 2-21)

- From a standing position, the athlete slowly begins moving his head side to side. As the movement becomes more comfortable, he should try to increase the range of motion of the movement, slowly tilting the head closer to each shoulder.

Figure 2-21. Head side to side

As the athlete becomes more efficient at performing each movement, the exercises can be performed in combinations. For example, the athlete can perform a knee tuck to a lunge walk, alternating legs after each movement has been performed. The combinations that can be created are nearly limitless. The primary advantage of combining movements is that it provides greater variety so that the flexibility-training program does not become monotonous. Combinations also create a more time-efficient program, because a larger number of muscle groups are stretched as opposed to when duplicating the same stretch repeatedly. This concept is important because many athletes have a limited amount of time to devote to their training programs.

3

Resistance Training

High levels of strength and power are necessary in the sport of football for both performance and injury-prevention demands.

The purpose of this chapter is to introduce the thought process behind developing successful strength and conditioning programs. Resistance training has come a long way from the days when the coach opened the doors and just let the athletes lift for an hour. A well-designed strength-training program can help develop a number of important physical characteristics that can be valuable in improving performance on the field.

Unfortunately, many football athletes frequently make the mistake of adhering to a bodybuilding program in an effort to improve sports performance. This mistake may occur because bodybuilding books or magazines are their primary sources of information, or because of the erroneous idea that because bodybuilders are so muscular they must be very strong and powerful.

Regardless of the reason, performing a bodybuilding program when the goal of training is improved football performance is a poor choice for several reasons. Most importantly, the only goal in bodybuilding is to increase muscle mass. The more muscular an individual is, the more successful he will be as a bodybuilder, because these athletes are evaluated strictly on appearance. Remind your players that bodybuilders don't need to be able to run, jump, twist, tackle, or throw.

Contrast that with the needs of a football player. First, appearance is of no importance. No points are awarded for being more muscular than the opposing team. The game is won based on the ability to carry out assignments more effectively than the opponents, to block and tackle more effectively, and perform the physical tasks that make up the game of football with more speed, quickness, and power than the opponent.

Some people might think that bodybuilders would be able to perform these football-related tasks at a very high performance level because they are so muscular. However, this assumption ignores a basic physiological principle: The changes that occur physiologically are specific to the demands of training. What does this mean to a football player? To reach an extreme level of muscularity, a bodybuilder must constantly maintain as much tension in the muscle as possible, meaning that all explosive or high-speed training must be avoided (Figure 3-1). In addition, a high number of repetitions must always be performed when the goal of training is hypertrophy. Unfortunately, the only way an individual can perform a high number of repetitions is to reduce the amount of weight being lifted. An athlete cannot achieve maximum strength and power while consistently performing slow-speed, moderate-intensity, high-volume training.

As just described, a bodybuilder always wants to lift slowly to maintain high levels of tension in the muscle tissue. However, a football athlete should include periods of higher-speed training to achieve optimal performance (Figure 3-2). It is important to remember that increases in strength occur primarily at the speed of training. What this means is that if an athlete always trains slowly he will get stronger at slower speeds, but his high-speed strength (i.e., power) will largely be unimproved. Because most movements in football occur at high speeds, getting stronger only at slow speeds is of little benefit in terms of improving performance.

Figure 3-1. To help athletes develop extreme levels of muscle hypertrophy, a bodybuilding program must avoid an emphasis on explosive weightlifting movements.

Figure 3-2. Explosive power is best developed with high-speed resistance-training movements such as cleans, jerks, or snatches.

Clearly, athletes should avoid utilizing exclusively bodybuilder-type training. Times may arise during the year when it is appropriate to use some training procedures seen in bodybuilding in the athletic strength and conditioning program. For the most part, however, the training program used to improve athletic performance should be far different than the training program Mr. Olympia uses in preparing for competition.

The Importance of Program Design

Designing effective resistance-training programs is critical to achieving optimal performance in football. You can run the most organized strength and conditioning facility in the country, own the best equipment, and have your athletes perform each exercise with perfect technique, but unless their programs are well thought out, structured, and organized so that the athletes reach a peak level of performance at the appropriate times, your strength and conditioning program will never be as effective as it should be.

For example, you may be a master at teaching your football players how to clean with perfect technique (Figure 3-3). But if you structure their program so that they are performing cleans with sets of eight repetitions, with 60 seconds between sets, and at the end of their workout, it does not matter how good their technique is because the effectiveness of the exercise has been severely compromised as a result of program design. It is more beneficial to be good at teaching correct exercise technique, but great at program design.

Figure 3-3. The ability to design effective resistance training programs is one of the most important qualities of a successful strength and conditioning coach.

The purpose of this section is to take you step by step through the process of designing an effective football resistance-training program. Football is a fall sport, with practice beginning in late July or early August and the season running into November or December as teams advance into playoffs or bowl games. Begin by setting a beginning date for off-season training. Provide your athletes with at least two weeks to recover physically and psychologically from the demands of competition. Because the athletes will have a difficult time training consistently during finals and Christmas break (unless you are participating in a bowl game), it makes more sense to resume training following Christmas break, early in January.

The start of practice in signals the conclusion of the off-season phase. Knowing the start and end dates of off-season training enables you to determine the number of weeks in the off-season training program (usually around 28 for a collegiate program).

The next variable to determine is the energy demands of the sport. Football is primarily a power sport, but the need for anaerobic endurance must also be addressed. Contrast this, for example, with throwing a shot put, which is all power, and running a marathon, which is highly aerobic in nature. The average play in football generally only takes about six seconds, but a collegiate football athlete may be on the field for 70 plays or more during a game, which is where the muscular-endurance component comes into play.

Because each football game is of equal importance (in contrast to a sport like track or swimming, where athletes peak for a specific meet), a need exists to try to bring the football athlete to a peak in power just before the start of the in-season phase, and then maintain that peak for the duration of the season. Thus, you must design your 28 weeks of off-season training to conclude with a cycle designed to maximally increase power.

After completing the in-season phase, the athletes may have two to four weeks or longer with no organized resistance training (depending on whether or not the team is participating in a bowl game). As a result, the athletes may begin off-season training in a mildly to moderately detrained state. To counter this situation, off-season training should begin with a short introduction cycle, made up of lower-volume, lower-intensity training to minimize muscular soreness. To summarize, off-season training should begin with an introduction cycle and conclude with a power cycle.

When the goal of training is to maximally increase power, it is advantageous to first increase strength levels because of the positive relationship between strength and power (Figure 3-4). Similarly, it is advantageous to increase muscle mass because of the positive relationship between muscle size and strength. Following the introduction cycle is the first strength cycle, made up of what would be considered high-repetition training, which is performed with a goal of increasing muscle mass. In addition, by starting with higher-repetition training, you can gradually increase the intensity of training as you progress through the off-season by decreasing the required number of repetitions. After initiating increases in muscle strength and size, you need to continue increasing strength levels (because of the relationship between strength and power), so it is a good idea to place a second consecutive strength cycle in the training program. Following these first two strength cycles, spring practice begins. During spring practice, revert to a training cycle similar to what the athletes perform in-season, reducing the volume of training but maintaining the intensity in an effort to maintain levels of strength and power. Following spring practice are two consecutive strength cycles designed to bring strength levels to a peak just prior to initiating two power cycles meant to maximize performance potential. The complete sequence of cycles and the length of each cycle should look something like this:
- Introduction—1 week
- Strength I—4 weeks
- Strength II—6 weeks

- Spring practice—4 weeks
- Strength III—3 weeks
- Strength IV—3 weeks
- Power I—4 weeks
- Power II—3 weeks

Figure 3-4. When the goal of training is to optimally increase power, it makes sense to first increase strength levels because of the relationship between strength and power.

Dividing the training cycles up in this manner provides a logical progression in terms of increasing power and making full use of the 28 weeks of off-season training. The cycles are sequenced so that each cycle builds off the previous one, bringing the athletes to a peak just prior to the start of the in-season phase.

The purpose of the introduction cycle is to reacquaint the athletes to the demands of resistance training. To accomplish this goal, the intensity guideline is based on performing the full number of repetitions in each set. The athletes each select a resistance that allows them to do this. This technique forces the athlete to use a moderate training resistance. The pace, or speed, of movement used during the introduction cycle is relatively slow, and the rest periods between sets and exercises are fairly long.

Exercise selection is based on training movements, not muscle groups. During resistance training, the increases in strength and power that occur are specific to the movement patterns that are used to perform the exercise. The more similar the exercise activity is to the movements that make up the sport, the more carry-over that occurs from the weight room to the playing field (Figure 3-5).

Figure 3-5. It is important to select exercises that mimic the positions and movement patterns that occur athletically. Therefore, players should perform as many exercises as possible from a standing position.

Exercise selection, like program design, should progress from general to specific. Therefore, as the off-season progresses, exercise selection should gradually become more and more specific to the movements that occur during competition. For example, it makes sense to perform a basic weightlifting exercise (e.g., push press) during the introductory cycle to develop strength and teach correct movement patterns. But as the off-season progresses, exercise selection should also progress. For example, in the power cycle that occurs just before the start of practice, the athletes could perform a series of dumbbell split, alternating foot–alternating arm jerks, which are an example of an exercise that is designed to develop power, coordination, and balance.

The order in which exercises are performed within each workout is also very important to overall program design. During each workout, weightlifting exercises should always be performed first for two reasons. First, these exercises are performed at a high rate of speed. That speed is compromised if athletes go into these exercises in a fatigued state, which would occur if they performed other exercises prior to performing the weightlifting exercises. Second, these exercises involve complex movement patterns, and the ability to perform complex movement patterns diminishes as fatigue sets in (Figure 3-6).

Weight-training exercises for the largest muscle group should always be performed first. For example, if pull-downs, squats, and leg curls are to be included in the workout, squats should be performed first because they involve more muscle-mass recruitment than do leg curls or pull-downs. Leg curls would be performed second and pull-downs third for the same reason.

Figure 3-6. It is important to perform the weightlifting movements early in the workout, when the athlete is not fatigued from the demands of the workout.

After the largest muscle group exercises have been performed, the trunk (i.e., the abdominals and low back) should be trained. Many exercisers train the trunk at the end of the workout. However, a strong trunk is critical for optimal athletic performance. Unfortunately, most athletes don't place a big enough emphasis on training the trunk, and if trunk training is not performed until the end of the workout many athletes will not perform the exercises with the necessary intensity. The intensity of these trunk exercises is enhanced if they are performed in the middle of the workout instead. Smaller muscle group exercises should be performed at the end of the workout, when energy levels are reduced. These exercises can be performed safely in a fatigued state.

After completion of the introduction cycle, the first of four strength cycles is initiated. During the strength cycles, several variables are adjusted from the training protocol used during the introduction cycle so that an increase in muscle strength can be achieved. First, the speed of movement is faster to allow greater training weights to be used (it is impossible to very slowly lift a heavy weight in a purposeful manner for the duration of the set). Next, as the training weight is increased, the number of repetitions is gradually decreased and the duration of rest periods is increased, which will allow for a greater training intensity. Note that the number of repetitions performed varies each week. For example, in strength cycle I, during weeks 1 and 3 the athletes perform core lifts at 4x9, but during weeks 2 and 4 core lifts are performed at 4x7.

Because athletes select their resistance based on their ability to complete the required number of repetitions (rather than performing exercises at a percentage of one-repetition maximum), adjusting the repetitions forces the athletes to vary the training resistance, and thereby vary the intensity of their training. During the introduction cycle, the intensity guideline instructs the athlete to select a resistance that allows for completion of the full number of required repetitions on each set.

In contrast, during the strength cycles the intensity guideline instructs the athlete to select a resistance that allows for completion of the full number of required repetitions on the first set only. Thus, while the workout may call for 4x5, in reality the athlete attempts to find a resistance with which he can complete five repetitions on the first set or two, but not for all four sets. This guideline allows the athlete to train with greater intensity, which is critical when the goal of training is increases in strength. It is also important that the athletes do not train to failure on each set. Instead, they should perform as many repetitions as they can on each set (within the repetition guidelines) with good form, and then discontinue the exercise if they are not going to be consistently spotted through any additional repetitions.

Workouts are further manipulated so that lower-volume training (i.e., 4x7 as compared to 4x9) is always completed at the end of the week when fatigue is highest. Therefore, athletes perform the higher-volume training early in the week (after not lifting Saturday and Sunday) and lower-volume training at the end of the week when fatigue from the week of training starts to accumulate. To accomplish this scenario and still vary the intensity at which they perform each exercise on a weekly basis requires further program manipulation.

For example, assume the athletes squat on Monday and bench press on Friday. The athletes would perform squats at 4x9 and bench at 4x7 for the duration of the cycle. This design does not provide the desired variation in training intensity. What is required is that the sequence that they perform during each workout varies each week. For example, athletes can train three days per week and alternate performing their Monday and Friday workouts as the first workout of the week. That is, during week 1, athletes perform the Monday workout on Monday and the Friday workout on Friday. During week 2, the Friday workout becomes the Monday workout and the Monday workout becomes the Friday workout. As a result, using this example, during week 1 the athletes perform squats at 4x9 and bench at 4x7. During week 2, because the sequence of workouts/days is alternated, they bench on Monday at 4x9 and perform squats on Friday at 4x7. Athletes lifting four days per week adhere to a similar protocol, pairing Monday/Thursday and Tuesday/Friday so that training intensity on each exercise varies weekly. The reason for this change is that exercise acts as a stress on the body, and the body adapts to this stress by getting stronger, more powerful, and more aerobically fit. However, the body is very good at adapting in an attempt to reduce that stress. By changing the workout sequence, you may reduce the body's ability to adapt to the stress of exercise. The goal is to keep stress levels at an optimum level and thereby also keep the physiological adaptations at an optimum level.

Following strength cycles I and II, the spring practice cycle is initiated. Focus on the two primary purposes of the spring practice cycle. The first is to maintain the increases in muscle size and strength that have occurred during the previous cycles. The spring practice cycle also serves to familiarize the athletes with the power and in-season cycles that occur later in the training year because the design and format of the spring practice cycle is similar to those cycles.

One of the primary program-design differences seen in the spring practice and in-season cycles is that the athletes are provided choices of exercises to perform rather than being told specifically what exercises to do. The reason for that is that during the spring practice and in-season cycles the athletes begin to accumulate minor injuries that may make it difficult to perform specific exercises. For example, a wrist injury may prevent an athlete from performing barbell cleans, but he can perform dumbbell cleans without aggravating the wrist injury. By providing choices of exercises, you enable your athletes to work around these injury situations.

The primary manipulations to the workout during the spring practice cycles are the introduction of percentage and timed exercises, which are used during the second of the two workouts completed each week. Because power is a combination of speed and force development, the emphasis should be on force development (strength) during the first workout of the week and speed development during the second workout of the week.

Percentages are assigned to the total-body exercises to allow for a greater movement speed and to most effectively maintain strength. Several studies have shown a minimum training intensity of 80 percent of one-repetition maximum (1 RM) is necessary to maintain strength and also allow a faster movement speed than what would occur at higher percentages. Therefore, athletes are required to train at a minimum of 80 percent of 1 RM while performing the weightlifting movements unless an injury situation prevents them from doing so. Timed exercises are exercises in which a time component has been added to the traditional set and rep scheme. Instruct your athletes to go as heavy as possible with their weight selection, but still complete the required number of repetitions in good form within the time allotted. This design has the effect of shifting the emphasis from how much athletes can lift to how quickly they can lift the resistance (Figure 3-7).

Figure 3-7. Timed exercises allow the emphasis to shift from how much can be lifted to how quickly the exercise can be performed.

After the spring practice cycle, athletes perform two consecutive strength cycles to bring strength levels to a peak. Because of the relationship between strength and power, it is advantageous to maximize strength levels before attempting to maximize power. To assist in optimizing increases in strength, the number of required repetitions is reduced and rest periods are increased.

To bring the athletes to a peak before the competition phase, two consecutive power cycles are then initiated. The performance demands of football require high power outputs. To place the emphasis on power development, percentage exercises and timed lifts are used to stress the rate of force development—similar to what occurs during the spring practice cycle. Exercise selection is very specific, and involves training those movements that make up the game of football.

At the completion of the two power cycles, the athletes are at a peak in terms of physical preparedness. With the start of practice, the emphasis in the weight room shifts to maintaining this physical peak. Because the athletes are spending a great deal of time and energy in practice, the number of workouts per week and the number of exercises within each workout are reduced, as are the number of sets performed. As during the spring practice cycle, the first workout of the week focuses on strength and the second workout concentrates on quick, explosive movements.

Athletes begin to accumulate various injuries that may hamper their ability to perform certain exercises during the in-season phase. Give them the opportunity to select which specific exercise they will perform during the in-season cycles. This technique allows them to train around injuries that might otherwise prevent them from completing their workouts.

Strength-Training Program Variables, Tools, and Protocols

A review of the thought process behind designing a resistance-training program for football has been presented. However, that information by itself does not give a complete picture of everything you should be trying to accomplish with the design of a resistance-training program. Simply increasing strength, and even power, in an athlete is not a difficult task. Unless the athlete has already achieved superior strength or power levels, most people with a basic understanding of strength-training principles could design a program that would result in increases in strength and/or power levels.

What is more challenging and more important is designing a resistance-training program that will increase functional levels of strength and power and improve various components of athleticism at the same time (Figure 3-8). The difference is significant because, except in the early- to mid-stages of developing an athlete, simply developing general strength will have very little positive effect on improving athletic performance. As a result, it is important to place a priority on designing training programs that develop the best possible athlete rather than simply maximal strength or power.

Figure 3-8. More important than simply increasing strength and power is developing *functional* strength and power that can be used to improve athletic performance.

The following variables will allow you to deviate from focusing solely on increasing strength and power levels and instead focus on improving athletic performance. Remember that the primary goal of any strength and conditioning program (except when training power lifters or weightlifters) needs to be improving athletic performance, not achieving maximal strength levels.

Training Weight

The most common method strength coaches use to program the amount of resistance to be used in an exercise is to determine or predict the one-repetition maximum in a particular exercise, and then have the athlete train at a percentage of that maximum. This method provides the strength and conditioning coach the opportunity to have greater control over the amount of resistance the athletes use while training.

In contrast, it is a good idea to have your athletes select their resistance based on their ability to complete the required number of repetitions. During the introductory and hypertrophy cycles, when you purposefully want to keep the volume of training high and the intensity moderate, instruct your athletes to select a resistance that will allow them to complete the full number of required repetitions while adhering to the specified rest times. To achieve the goal of completing the full number of repetitions in each set, especially during the hypertrophy cycle when rest times are short, instruct the athletes to reduce the weight by set, or even midset, to achieve the desired volume of training. When the athlete can complete the full number of required repetitions in each set, the resistance is increased.

During the strength cycles, and in certain exercises during the power cycles, instruct the athletes to select a resistance that allows for completion of the full number of required repetitions on the first set only (Figure 3-9). This technique allows the athlete, after warming up, to use as heavy a resistance as possible while still being able to

Figure 3-9. When training to increase strength, the critical aspect of program design is the intensity of training.

complete the required number of repetitions in good form on the first set. By adhering to the proper rest period, the athlete may be able to duplicate this effort on the second set, but generally from the third set on, if the weight was selected correctly, the number of repetitions the athlete is able to complete in good form decreases.

This design eliminates the need for frequent testing, which is important because of the large number of athletes on a football team. Furthermore, it gets away from a one-size-fits-all mentality in which every athlete is supposed to get the same training response from performing a certain number of repetitions at a particular percentage of his one-repetition maximum. Athletes have different abilities; some athletes may be able to easily perform the required number of repetitions at a given percentage while others may find it a more significant challenge. By allowing the athletes to select their training weight based on their individual capabilities, you allow each of your athletes to train at an intensity that is right for his specific physiological responses and abilities. This design also gives part of the ownership of the training intensity to the athlete, which in the vast majority of cases has a very positive effect.

Straps

The use of straps is common among power lifters, weightlifters, and bodybuilders. Straps can certainly play an important role in those types of activities. However, they do not belong in an athletic weight room. Until your opponents start wearing uniforms with straps attached to them, you should not allow your athletes to use them in training. Does this limit an athlete's ability to handle heavy weights? Initially, yes it can. The limiting factor in an athlete's ability to perform an exercise may be his grip strength. However, this problem is quickly overcome through training. You want your athletes, regardless of position, to have tremendous grip strength, and eliminating the use of straps will help you accomplish that goal.

Partials

If you are interested in constantly making your program better, one thing that you need to be able to do is incorporate new ideas into your training programs. If you learn of a training technique that can have a positive effect on your athletes' performance capabilities, you need to be willing to work it into the training program. Partials are a technique that may have an immediate impact on your players' performance levels. When performing a set of partials, the athlete lowers the weight at a normal speed of movement. Somewhere within the range of motion of the descent phase his partner counts off the repetition number. As soon as the athlete hears this, he moves from the lowering phase to the lifting phase as quickly as possible. This technique goes against the normal line of thinking, which states that you should always go through the entire range of motion of each exercise. Performing the exercise through the full range of motion makes sense when the goal is maximal strength, muscle size, or general fitness. However, in many sports activities the ability to transition as quickly as possible from an eccentric contraction to a concentric contraction, at any point in the range of motion, can have important performance-enhancing effects.

Training for Power

When training for football (and actually for most sports), increasing muscular power should be the primary goal (Figure 3-10). In football, the ability to produce high-speed strength (i.e., power) is a key component of successful performance. While a relationship exists between strength and power, training only for maximum strength will not lead to maximum increases in power. Power is a separate component, and the training program must be adjusted when the emphasis shifts from developing strength to developing power. The following four components (weightlifting–style lifts, timed exercises, percentage exercises, and plyometric exercises) can be introduced into the training program to assist with this shifting emphasis.

Figure 3-10. When training to improve performance in football, increasing power is more important than simply increasing strength levels. Increases in power can occur through both barbell and dumbbell training, especially when emphasizing the weightlifting movements.

Weightlifting-Style Lifts

To increase power capabilities, emphasize performance of weightlifting-style exercises. Research has shown that power output when performing such exercises (e.g., cleans, snatches) can be very high. Because of this increased power output, and because the movement pattern that occurs when performing these types of exercises is similar to the movement patterns seen in football (e.g., blocking and tackling), it makes sense to make the weightlifting-style exercises a priority in the training program.

Timed Exercises

Timed lifts can also be used to increase power (Figure 3-11). During a timed exercise, a specific amount of time is given to perform the required number of repetitions. The athlete is instructed to use as much weight as possible but still complete the required number of repetitions in the specified time period, shifting the emphasis from how much can be lifted to how quickly it can be lifted. The actual movement speed may not be especially fast, but the intent to move the resistance as quickly as possible is constantly emphasized.

Figure 3-11. Timed lifts can also be used to increase high-speed strength, or power.

Because the actual movement speed may not be excessively fast, the athlete is not forced to slow the bar or dumbbell down over a large portion of the range of motion, as is frequently seen with low resistances performed at high speeds. Again, emphasize the intent to move the weight very quickly, though the actual movement speed is not necessarily extremely fast. As with other types of training, emphasize the maintenance of good technique during timed exercises.

Percentage Exercises

Programming a percentage of one-repetition maximum (1 RM) on selected exercises can also help develop power. While it has been determined that the highest power outputs during weight training occur at 30 percent of 1 RM, the percentage used depends on the sport and the demands of the position. For volleyball athletes, where speed is more important than force development, a percentage as low as 30 percent 1 RM can be used. For football players, where force development plays an important role in performance, the percentage may range from 50 percent (kickers) to 80 percent (offensive/defensive linemen) of 1 RM. Utilizing a lower percentage of 1 RM allows for a faster training velocity, which more closely mimics the speeds of movement that occur during competition.

Plyometric Exercises

Plyometric training should also be emphasized when the goal is to increase power. However, it is important to select plyometric drills that are movement-specific (i.e., as with resistance training, plyometric drills should be selected based on their similarity to movements that occur within the sport). In this manner, plyometric training can be used to link increases in strength to improved movement capabilities. If the athlete's ability to move effectively during competition is enhanced as a result of training, then the training program has achieved the desired goal of enhancing performance.

Train Movements, Not Muscles

Remember, resistance training is movement-specific (i.e., increases in strength or power levels occur in the specific movement patterns used in training). Therefore, increasing strength/power levels in a movement pattern that is dissimilar to the movements that occur in football is of little value. For example, leg extensions and leg presses are effective at increasing the size and strength of the quadriceps (Figure 3-12). However, when performing these exercises, the athlete is increasing strength levels with a movement pattern that is not sport-specific. As a result, the value of performing leg extensions or leg presses for football athletes is minimal at best. Contrast that with exercises such as squats and lunges, which are also effective at increasing the size and strength levels in the quadriceps (among other muscle groups), and are performed in a movement pattern that is similar to movements seen in football. Clearly, squats and lunges are better choices than leg extensions or leg presses for football athletes. This same thought process needs to be applied when selecting exercises for the entire workout.

Figure 3-12. Increasing strength or power using exercises (such as leg extensions and leg presses) that involve a movement pattern dissimilar to what occurs on the football field is of little value in terms of improving performance.

Multijoint, Closed-Kinetic-Chain Exercises

For the football athlete, all movements making up the sport occur in a standing position. Furthermore, all movement that occurs in football involves movement around more than one joint. Because the adaptations that occur as a result of training are specific to the imposed demands, it makes sense that a majority of resistance-training movements involve standing, multijoint exercises (Figure 3-13). Remember, the more specific the training is to the demands of football, the better the transfer effect will be from training to performance enhancement. For example, football athletes should supplement the traditional bench press exercise with a standing bench press, because it takes the athlete out of a laying position and places him into a more sport-specific standing position (Figure 3-14).

Figure 3-13. A majority of the resistance-training movements in an athletic resistance-training program should be standing, multijoint, closed kinetic-chain exercises.

Figure 3-14. Performing a standing bench press movement takes the athlete out of non-sport-specific position and gets him on his feet, into a more functional position.

The primary exceptions to this rule are exercises included in the training program to reduce the risk of injury or to maintain muscular balance. For example, manual resistance-training movements for the neck are performed in a seated position and involve movement at only one joint. Other exercises, such as pull-downs or seated rows, are generally performed from a seated position. However, these types of exercises are the exception rather than the rule.

Dumbbell Exercises

If the goal of training is to maximally increase the ability to demonstrate strength with a barbell, then dumbbells should be used very little, if at all. That is why weightlifters and power lifters perform very few, if any, dumbbell exercises. On the other hand, if the goal of the training program is to enhance athletic performance, then dumbbells should make up a significant portion of the training program (Figure 3-15). The balance and body control required to perform dumbbell exercises is elevated, which makes them a great choice when training football athletes. Dumbbells require a greater level of balance, body control, and stabilization than do barbells, and these aspects transfer very well to the demands of football.

Figure 3-15. If the goal of training is to improve athletic performance, dumbbell training should make up a significant portion of the training program.

One good program-design idea is to have your skill-position athletes—quarterbacks, running backs, fullbacks, wide receivers, and defensive backs—perform resistance training during the off-season on Monday, Wednesday, and Friday, with Wednesday being their dumbbell-training day. This workout is a total-body training workout, meaning that they perform both lower- and upper-body exercises with dumbbells each Wednesday. All other positions—including offensive linemen, defensive linemen, and linebackers—can lift Monday, Tuesday, Thursday, and Friday, with the sequence in which they perform dumbbell training varying with each cycle.

Alternating Exercises

Dumbbells also provide the opportunity to perform alternating-limb upper-body exercises (e.g., alternating dumbbell cleans, alternating dumbbell bench press) (Figure 3-16). These types of exercises cannot be performed with a barbell. The advantage of performing alternating dumbbell exercises is that they provide a more sport-specific mode of training for football athletes. Think of a running back carrying the ball in one arm and straight-arming a would-be tackler with the other, or a linebacker fighting off a block with one arm while assisting on a tackle with the other. Alternating dumbbell exercises provide the opportunity to more closely mimic what occurs in competition, thereby increasing the degree of training specificity.

Figure 3-16. Dumbbells provide the opportunity to perform alternating-limb upper-body exercises, providing a sport-specific mode of training for the football athlete.

Manual Resistance

Emphasize multijoint dynamic training throughout the training year. However, during the hypertrophy cycle, make use of manual-resistance training (Figure 3-17). This slow-speed, high-intensity training fits in nicely with the goal of training for muscular hypertrophy. Similar to dumbbell training, it also provides variety in your training program. Furthermore, it builds mental toughness, because you can design your manual-resistance workouts to be very physically challenging. Most athletes respond to this challenge with tremendous enthusiasm.

You can also make occasional use of manual-resistance exercises throughout the training year as a change of pace for your athletes. For example, have your athletes perform certain supplemental exercises with manual resistance, such as upright rows or biceps curls.

Split Positions

Typically, standing exercises are performed with a shoulder-width stance, as in cleans, squats, and shoulder presses. Relatively few exercises are performed in a split position,

Figure 3-17. Manual resistance training is a high intensity, mentally challenging training mode that can be integrated into the training program.

which is important to note, because athletes spend a portion of their time on the field in a split position. Because the athletes will get stronger in the specific positions in which they train, they should perform certain exercises in a split position, alternating the forward foot with each repetition.

Single-Leg Exercises

Single-leg support exercises are important when running is a part of the activity (including football) because, while running, the athlete is predominantly in a single-leg support position (Figure 3-18). Single-leg exercises are also important in contact sports such as football, in which athletes are put into a single-leg support position after being knocked off balance by an opponent. By increasing strength levels in these single-leg support positions, the football athlete is better prepared for the demands of competition, providing them a potential competitive edge.

Lateral Movements

Most weight-training movements occur in the sagittal plane. Exercises such as cleans, squats, and lunges all occur in this plane. In contrast, football is a mixture of straight-ahead and lateral movements (Figure 3-19). Examples include a running back making a quick lateral movement to avoid a tackle or an offensive tackle making a quick lateral movement to pass block the defensive end.

Figure 3-18. Single-leg exercises are important in sports that involve running or contact where the athlete is put into a single-leg support position.

Figure 3-19. Football, and in fact most sports, are a combination of linear and lateral movements. Therefore, it is important to include both linear and lateral resistance-training movements in the resistance-training program.

If athletes only train in the sagittal plane, they are not preparing for optimal lateral-movement capabilities. To meet this need for lateral movement, athletes should perform a variety of lateral-training movements, both in the weight room and when plyometric/agility training. If a movement occurs on the field and that movement can be safely trained in the weight room, it should be included in the workout. To neglect lateral training is a disservice to your athletes.

Power Zone Emphasis

Many athletes make the mistake of training the arms and legs first while either ignoring or placing a lesser emphasis on strengthening the core (or power zone) of the body (Figure 3-20). The downside of this technique is that all movement is initiated at the core. If an athlete is lacking a strong core, optimal athletic performance cannot occur.

Figure 3-20. Many athletes place a great emphasis on training the limbs, but ignore the importance of training the core, which is unfortunate because optimal athletic performance cannot occur without a well-developed core.

The core is much more than the abdominal muscles. In addition to the abdominals (i.e., the rectus abdominis, external obliques, internal obliques, and transverse abdominis), the core consists of the following muscle groups:
- Hip musculature: psoas, gluteus medius and maximus, and adductors
- Lumbar spine musculature: multifidus, interspinalis, intertransversarii, rotators, quadratus lumborum, and deep and superficial erector spinae
- Thoracic spine musculature: transverospinalis muscles, lower/middle trapezius, rhomboids, and serratus anterior/posterior
- Cervical spine musculature: paraspinalis, scalenes, sternocleidomastoid, and longus coli and capitis

Performing trunk training in the middle of the workout rather than at the end can be advantageous because athletes may train the area with more intensity. Like other muscle groups, exercise selection for the trunk should be cycled, beginning with basic exercises (e.g., crunches, toe touches) and gradually working toward more demanding sport-specific exercises (e.g., medicine-ball single-leg twisting throws, medicine-ball single-leg overhead throws). Placing a significant emphasis on training the low back is also important. Use exercises such as back extensions, glute ham raises, and Romanian dead lifts to strengthen this area.

Rotational Movements

Football involves rotational movement (e.g., throwing, twisting off a block or tackle). However, many coaches tend to undertrain rotational movements. Because rotational movement occurs in competition, it is critical to train rotational movement in the weight room and in plyometric/agility training (Figure 3-21). Athletes should be fully prepared for any rotational movements they may have to perform in competition, so it is essential that you include rotational movements in your training programs.

Figure 3-21. Because rotational movements occur frequently during competition, it is important to include rotational movements in the training program.

Strongman Implements

Another training variable that you can introduce into your football strength and conditioning program is the use of training implements typically associated with strongman competitions. As a strength and conditioning coach, it is important that you remember what it is you are trying to accomplish with your strength and conditioning program. Your two primary goals should be to improve athletic performance and reduce injury potential. As long as the training regimens you provide to your athletes assist in accomplishing those goals, you should be open to implementing new ideas into your program.

It is common for strength and conditioning coaches to make use of exercises and training procedures that are derived from the sports of powerlifting and weightlifting. Likewise, techniques used in strongman events may transfer well to the training programs of football athletes. It is important to remember to take only those portions of the discipline that apply to football and disregard the rest. In other words, don't train your football players as weightlifters. Train them as football players, but make use of some of the weightlifting exercises in their training programs. However, they should also perform a variety of exercises (e.g., lateral squats, pull-downs) that would not commonly be performed by weightlifters. Similarly, your athletes should perform some exercises with implements that would typically be seen in a strongman competition, but with a constant emphasis on enhanced performance.

A good example of integrating strongman training into your training programs is the use of water-filled barrels (Figure 3-22). Using water as resistance provides a unique advantage for football athletes because water provides an active, fluid resistance rather

Figure 3-22. Strongman implements can be integrated into the football resistance-training program to provide a performance advantage and provide variation in the training program.

than a static resistance. As the athlete performs the exercise, the water constantly moves within the barrel. In contrast, a typical exercise using either a weight stack on a machine or free weights provides a much more static resistance.

Unfortunately, little if any research has been done evaluating the value of training with a fluid resistance. But, applying the concept of specificity, it would seem that training with a fluid resistance is a more sport-specific method of training, because, in most situations, athletes more commonly encounter dynamic resistance (in the form of an opponent). In addition, because the active fluid resistance increases the need for stability, this type of training may reduce the chance for injury by improving joint stability.

You can also use large truck or tractor tires in your resistance-training programs. The tires should be used primarily on days when the athletes are performing dumbbell cleans. The athletes can be given the option of substituting one or more sets of dumbbell cleans with tire flips. Flipping the tire provides advantages to your athletes, including:
- Greater variation in required exercises
- Less stress on the joints because the athletes are only flipping the tire, not catching it as they would in an weightlifting movement
- The ability to focus on explosiveness, because less technique is involved than when completing an weigh lifting–style lift

The Workouts

The workouts you develop should be divided into positions—offensive linemen/tight ends, running backs/wide receivers, fullbacks, quarterbacks, kickers, defensive linemen/linebackers, and defensive backs—for two reasons. First, by dividing the workouts this way you can create more sport-specific workouts. For example, the position demands of an offensive lineman are different than the position demands of a kicker or a defensive back, so why give them the same workout to perform?

The other primary benefit of dividing the workouts up into positions is that it allows you to use your strength and conditioning facility more effectively. For example, on Monday and Friday the entire team can be in the facility at the same time. On Tuesday and Thursday, the skill-position athletes perform speed/plyometric training, so only the offensive linemen/tight ends, fullbacks, and defensive linemen/linebackers are lifting weights. On Wednesday and Saturday, the offensive linemen/tight ends, fullbacks, and defensive linemen/linebackers perform speed/plyometric training, so only the skill-position athletes are lifting weights. Because you want your athletes to perform the workout in the programmed order, you may end up having athletes waiting for equipment if all positions performed the same workout on the same day. To avoid this scenario, design your workouts so that a portion of the team performs a barbell-oriented workout while the remaining athletes perform a dumbbell-oriented workout. This design has the effect of spreading the athletes throughout the weight room so that the facility is used more efficiently.

The training cycles provided here are for both the skill-position and non-skill-position athletes. These training cycles provide the framework upon which the resistance-training programs are designed. Following the training cycles, sample workouts from each cycle for both skill-position athletes and non-skill-position athletes are presented so that you can see how these workouts are put together and understand the differences in program design for these two position groups. The workouts shown are representative of what is recommended and should be used as guidelines in developing your own workouts based on your situation. The cycles are presented in chronological order, with one sample workout offered for each cycle. The player position used for each cycle varies.

Glossary of Abbreviations

The following abbreviations are used throughout the sample workouts in this chapter.

AL = Auxiliary lift (any single-joint exercise, such as a biceps curl or leg extension)
ALT = Alternate
CL = Core lift (any multijoint exercise, such as a squat or bench press)
CMD = Command
DB = Dumbbell
EZ = Easy curl bar
FLR = Floor (the exercise is initiated from the floor)
FT = Foot
MB = Medicine ball
MR = Manual resistance (the exercise is performed with a partner providing manual resistance)
NG = Narrow grip
PD = Pull-down
RDL = Romanian dead lift
SLDL = Straight-leg dead lift
TB = Total body (any of the weightlifting–style exercises or associated training lifts)
TL = Timed lift
WT = Weight

Training Cycles

Skill-Position Athletes

DATES: Nov 25–Jan 5
CYCLE: Pre-Introduction (freshmen only)
GOAL: Introduce athletes to the demands of resistance training and emphasize correct technique.
LENGTH: 6 weeks
INTENSITY: Select a resistance that allows for completion of the full number of required repetitions on *each* set prior to increasing resistance.
PACE: Perform total-body lifts explosively. For all other exercises, lift in 2 seconds and lower in 4 seconds.
REST: 2:00 between sets and exercises
SETS/REPS:
- Nov 25–Dec 1: TB=3x7, CL=3x11, AL=3x11
- Dec 2–Dec 8: TB=3x4, CL=3x8, AL=3x8
- Dec 9–Dec 10: TB=3x7, CL=3x11, AL=3x11
- Dec 16–Dec 22: TB=3x4, CL=3x8, AL=3x8
- Dec 23–Dec 29: TB=3x7, CL=3x11, AL=3x11
- Dec 30–Jan 5: TB=3x4, CL=3x8, AL=3x8

DATES: Jan 6–Jan 12
CYCLE: Introduction
GOAL: Reintroduce athletes to the demands of resistance training and emphasize correct technique.
LENGTH: 1 week
INTENSITY: Select a resistance that allows for completion of the full number of required repetitions on *each* set prior to increasing resistance.
PACE: Perform total-body lifts explosively. For all other exercises, lift in 2 seconds and lower in 4 seconds.
REST: 2:00 between sets and exercises
SETS/REPS:
- Jan 6–Jan 12: TB=3x5, CL=3x8, AL=3x8

DATES: Jan 13–Feb 9
CYCLE: Strength I
GOAL: Increase muscle size, because of the positive relationship between muscle strength and power.
LENGTH: 4 weeks
INTENSITY: Select a resistance that allows for completion of the full number of required repetitions on *each* set prior to increasing resistance.
PACE: Perform total-body lifts explosively. For all other exercises, lift in 2 seconds and lower in 3 seconds.
REST: 2:00 between all sets and exercises
SETS/REPS:
- Jan 13–Jan 19: TB=4x6, CL=4x9, AL=3x9
- Jan 20–Jan 26: TB=4x4, CL=4x7, AL=3x7

- Jan 27–Feb 2: TB=4x6, CL=4x9, AL=3x9
- Feb 3–Feb 9: TB=4x4, CL=4x7, AL=3x7

DATES: Feb 10–March 23
CYCLE: Strength II
GOAL: Further increase muscle strength, because of the positive relationship between strength and power.
LENGTH: 6 weeks
INTENSITY: Select a resistance that allows for completion of the full number of required repetitions on the *first* set only prior to increasing resistance.
PACE: Perform total-body lifts explosively. For all other exercises, lift in 2 seconds and lower in 3 seconds.
REST: 2:30 between total-body exercises, 2:00 between all other sets and exercises
SETS/REPS:
- Feb 10–Feb 17: TB=4x5, CL=4x6, AL=3x6
- Feb 18–Feb 24: TB=4x3, CL=4x4, AL=3x6
- Feb 25–March 3: TB=4x5, CL=4x6, AL=3x6
- March 4–March 10: TB=4x3, CL=4x4, AL=3x6
- March 11–March 12: TB=4x5, CL=4x6, AL=3x6
- March 13–March 23: TB=4x3, CL=4x4, AL=3x6

DATES: March 31–April 27
CYCLE: Spring Practice
GOAL: Increase muscle power, because of the positive relationship between muscle power and performance.
LENGTH: 4 weeks
INTENSITY: For total-body exercises, select a resistance that allows for completion of the full number of required repetitions on the *first* set only prior to increasing resistance. For timed exercises, reduce the resistance as necessary to maintain the desired speed of movement during each set.
PACE: Perform total-body lifts explosively. Perform timed lifts at a pace that allows for completion of the required number of repetitions in the specified time period.
REST: 3:00 between total-body exercises, 2:30 between all other sets and exercises
SETS/REPS:
(The number is parentheses represents the number of seconds to be spent performing each repetition. For example, during the first week, performing 3 repetitions at a pace of 1.2 seconds per repetition requires a set duration of approximately 4 seconds.)
- March 31–April 6: TB=3x2, TL=3x3@4 sec (1.2)
- April 7–April 13: TB=3x4, TL=3x6@9 sec (1.5)
- April 14–April 20: TB=3x2, TL=3x3@4 sec (1.2)
- April 21–April 27: TB=3x4, TL=3x6@9 sec (1.5)

DATES: April 28–May 18
CYCLE: Strength III
GOAL: Further increase muscle strength, because of the positive relationship between strength and power.
LENGTH: 3 weeks

INTENSITY: Select a resistance that allows for completion of the full number of required repetitions on the *first* set only prior to increasing resistance.
PACE: Perform total-body lifts. For all other exercises, lift in 2 seconds and lower in 3 seconds.
REST: 2:30 between total-body exercises, 2:00 between all other sets and exercises
SETS/REPS:
- April 28–May 5: TB=4x3, CL=4x3, AL=3x8
- May 6–May 12: TB=4x4, CL=4x5, AL=3x8
- May 13–May 18: TB=4x3, CL=4x3, AL=3x8

DATES: May 19–June 8
CYCLE: Strength IV
GOAL: Further increase muscle strength, because of the positive relationship between strength and power.
LENGTH: 3 weeks
INTENSITY: Select a resistance that allows for completion of the full number of required repetitions on the *first* set only prior to increasing resistance.
PACE: Perform total-body lifts explosively. For all other exercises, lift in 2 seconds and lower in 3 seconds.
REST: 2:30 between total-body exercises, 2:00 between all other sets and exercises
SETS/REPS:
- May 19–May 25: TB=4x4, CL=4x4, AL=3x6
- May 26–June 2: TB=4x2, CL=4x2, AL=3x6
- June 3–June 8: TB=4x4, CL=4x4, AL=3x6

DATES: June 9–July 6
CYCLE: Power I
GOAL: Increase muscle power, because of the positive relationship between muscle power and performance.
LENGTH: 4 weeks
INTENSITY: For total-body exercises, select a resistance that allows for completion of the full number of required repetitions on the *first* set only prior to increasing resistance. For timed exercises, reduce the resistance as necessary to maintain the desired speed of movement during each set.
PACE: Perform total-body lifts explosively. Timed lifts should be performed at a pace that allows for completion of the required number of repetitions in the specified time period.
REST: 3:00 between total-body exercises, 2:30 between all other sets and exercises
SETS/REPS:
- June 9–June 15: TB=5x3, TL=4x6@9 sec (1.5)
- June 16–June 22: TB=5x3, TL=4x3@4 sec (1.2)
- June 23–June 29: TB=5x3, TL=4x6@9 sec (1.5)
- June 30–July 6: TB=5x2, TL=4x3@4 sec (1.2)

DATES: July 7–July 27
CYCLE: Power II
GOAL: Further increase muscle power, because of the positive relationship between muscle power and performance.

LENGTH: 3 weeks
INTENSITY: For total-body exercises, select a resistance that allows for completion of the full number of required repetitions on the *first* set only prior to increasing resistance. For timed exercises, reduce the resistance as necessary to maintain the desired speed of movement during each set.
PACE: Perform total-body lifts explosively. Timed lifts should be performed at a pace that allows for completion of the required number of repetitions in the specified time period. For all other exercises, lift in 2 seconds and lower in 3 seconds.
REST: 3:00 between total-body exercises, 2:30 between all other sets and exercises
SETS/REPS:
- July 7–July 13: TB=5x3, TL=4x4@6 sec (1.5)
- July 14–July 20: TB=5x2, TL=4x2@2 sec (1)
- July 21–July 27: TB=5x1, TL=4x2@2 sec (1)

DATES: July 28–Sept 7
CYCLE: In-Season I
GOAL: Increase strength and power during the competitive season.
LENGTH: 6 weeks
INTENSITY: Select a resistance that allows for completion of the full number of required repetitions on the *first* set only prior to increasing resistance.
PACE: Perform total-body lifts explosively. For all other exercises, lift in 1.5 seconds and lower in 2 seconds.
REST: 2:00 between total-body exercises, 1:30 between all other sets and exercises
SETS/REPS:
- July 28–Aug 3: TB=3x2, CL=3x3, AL=3x5
- Aug 4–Aug 10: TB=3x4, CL=3x5, AL=3x5
- Aug 11–Aug 17: TB=3x2, CL=3x3, AL=3x5
- Sept 18–Aug 24: TB=3x4, CL=3x5, AL=3x5
- Aug 25–Aug 31: TB=3x2, CL=3x3, AL=3x5
- Sept 1–Sept 7: TB=3x4, CL=3x5, AL=3x5

DATES: Sept 8–Oct 19
CYCLE: In-Season II
GOAL: Increase strength and power during the competitive season.
LENGTH: 6 weeks
INTENSITY: Select a resistance that allows for completion of the full number of required repetitions on the *first* set only prior to increasing resistance.
PACE: Perform total-body lifts explosively. For all other exercises, lift in 1.5 seconds and lower in 2 seconds.
REST: 2:30 between total-body exercises, 2:00 between all other sets and exercises
SETS/REPS:
- Sept 8–Sept 13: TB=3x3, CL=3x2, AL=3x5
- Sept 14–Sept 20: TB=3x5, CL=3x4, AL=3x5
- Sept 21–Sept 27: TB=3x3, CL=3x2, AL=3x5
- Sept 28–Oct 5: TB=3x5, CL=3x4, AL=3x5
- Oct 6–Oct 12: TB=3x3, CL=3x2, AL=3x5
- Oct 13–Oct 19: TB=3x5, CL=3x4, AL=3x5

DATES: Oct 20–Nov 22
CYCLE: In-Season III
GOAL: Increase strength and power during the competitive season.
LENGTH: 5 weeks
INTENSITY: Select a resistance that allows for completion of the full number of required repetitions on the *first* set only prior to increasing resistance.
PACE: Perform total-body lifts explosively. For all other exercises, lift in 1.5 seconds and lower in 2 seconds.
REST: 2:30 between total-body exercises, 2:00 between all other sets and exercises
SETS/REPS:
- Oct 20–Oct 26: TB=3x2, CL=3x3, AL=3x5
- Oct 26–Nov 2: TB=3x4, CL=3x5, AL=3x5
- Nov 3–Nov 9: TB=3x2, CL=3x3, AL=3x5
- Nov 10–Nov 16: TB=3x4, CL=3x5, AL=3x5
- Nov 17–Nov 22: TB=3x2, CL=3x3, AL=3x5

Pre-Introduction Cycle

QUARTERBACKS

Monday/Friday*

DATES: Nov 25–Jan 5
CYCLE: Pre-Introduction (freshmen only)
GOAL: Introduce athletes to the demands of resistance training and emphasize correct technique.
LENGTH: 6 weeks
INTENSITY: Select a resistance that allows for completion of the full number of required repetitions on *each* set prior to increasing resistance.
PACE: Perform total-body lifts. For all other exercises, lift in 2 seconds and lower in 4 seconds.
REST: 2:00 between sets and exercises
SETS/REPS:
- Nov 25–Dec 1: TB=3x7, CL=3x11, AL=3x11
- Dec 2–Dec 8: TB=3x4, CL=3x8, AL=3x8
- Dec 9–Dec 15: TB=3x7, CL=3x11, AL=3x11
- Dec 16–Dec 22: TB=3x4, CL=3x8, AL=3x8
- Dec 23–Dec 29: TB=3x7, CL=3x11, AL=3x11
- Dec 30–Jan 5: TB=3x4, CL=3x8, AL=3x8

* As noted in the "Importance of Program Design" section earlier in this chapter, the Monday and Friday workouts alternate each week. The workout performed on Monday during week 1 is performed on Friday during week 2, and vice versa.

	Week 1 MON	Week 2 FRI	Week 3 MON	Week 4 FRI	Week 5 MON	Week 6 FRI
TOTAL BODY Push Press TB WT Lifted	3x7 ____	3x4 ____	3x7 ____	3x4 ____	3x7 ____	3x4 ____
LOWER BODY Squats CL WT Lifted Lunges CL (Total) WT Lifted	3x11 ____ 3x11 ____	3x8 ____ 3x8 ____	3x11 ____ 3x11 ____	3x8 ____ 3x8 ____	3x11 ____ 3x11 ____	3x8 ____ 3x8 ____
TRUNK WT Crunch WT Lifted WT Twist Crunch WT Lifted WT Back Extension WT Lifted	3x20 ____ 3x20 ____ 3x15 ____	3x20 ____ 3x20 ____ 3x15 ____	3x20 ____ 3x20 ____ 3x15 ____	3x20 ____ 3x20 ____ 3x15 ____	3x20 ____ 3x20 ____ 3x15 ____	3x20 ____ 3x20 ____ 3x15 ____
UPPER BACK Seated Row/PD/T-Bar CL WT Lifted	3x11 ____	3x8 ____	3x11 ____	3x8 ____	3x11 ____	3x8 ____
ROTATOR CUFF Functional Rotation Reps Completed Internal Rotation Reps Completed	2x12 ____ 2x12 ____	2x12 ____ 2x12 ____	2x12 ____ 2x12 ____	2x12 ____ 2x12 ____	2x12 ____ 2x12 ____	2x12 ____ 2x12 ____

Monday/Friday Workout Regimen

Wednesday

DATES: Nov 25–Jan 5
CYCLE: Pre-Introduction (freshmen only)
GOAL: Introduce athletes to the demands of resistance training and emphasize correct technique.
LENGTH: 6 weeks
INTENSITY: Select a resistance that allows for completion of the full number of required repetitions on *each* set prior to increasing resistance.
PACE: Perform total-body lifts explosively. For all other exercises, lift in 2 seconds and lower in 4 seconds.
REST: 2:00 between sets and exercises
SETS/REPS:

- Nov 25–Dec 1: TB=3x4, CL=3x8, AL=3x8
- Dec 2–Dec 8: TB=3x7, CL=3x11, AL=3x11
- Dec 9–Dec 15: TB=3x4, CL=3x8, AL=3x8
- Dec 16–Dec 22: TB=3x7, CL=3x11, AL=3x11
- Dec 23–Dec 29: TB=3x4, CL=3x8, AL=3x8
- Dec 30–Jan 5: TB=3x7, CL=3x11, AL=3x11

	Week 1	Week 2	Week 3	Week 4	Week 5	Week 6
TOTAL BODY DB Squat Clean (Shin) TB WT Lifted	3x4 ____	3x7 ____	3x4 ____	3x7 ____	3x4 ____	3x7 ____
LOWER BODY DB Squats CL WT Lifted	3x8 ____	3x11 ____	3x8 ____	3x11 ____	3x8 ____	3x11 ____
Leg Curl/MR Leg Curl AL WT Lifted	3x8/2x8 ____	3x11/2x8 ____	3x8/2x8 ____	3x11/2x8 ____	3x8/2x8 ____	3x11/2x8 ____
TRUNK WT ALT Toe Touch WT Lifted	3x20 ____	3x20 ____	3x20 ____	3x20 ____	3x20 ____	3x20 ____
WT Twist Back Extension WT Lifted	3x15 ____	3x15 ____	3x15 ____	3x15 ____	3x15 ____	3x15 ____
CHEST/SHOULDER DB Incline Press CL WT Lifted	3x8 ____	3x11 ____	3x8 ____	3x11 ____	3x8 ____	3x11 ____
DB Front Raise AL WT Lifted	3x8 ____	3x11 ____	3x8 ____	3x11 ____	3x8 ____	3x11 ____
NECK MR Flexion/Extension Reps Completed	2x8 ____	2x8 ____	2x8 ____	2x8 ____	2x8 ____	2x8 ____

Wednesday Workout Regimen

Friday/Monday

DATES: Nov 25–Jan 5
CYCLE: Pre-Introduction (freshmen only)
GOAL: Introduce athletes to the demands of resistance training and emphasize correct technique.
LENGTH: 6 weeks
INTENSITY: Select a resistance that allows for completion of the full number of required repetitions on *each* set prior to increasing resistance.
PACE: Perform total-body lifts explosively. For all other exercises, lift in 2 seconds and lower in 4 seconds.
REST: 2:00 between sets and exercises
SETS/REPS:
- Nov 25–Dec 1: TB=3x7, CL=3x11, AL=3x11
- Dec 2–Dec 8: TB=3x4, CL=3x8, AL=3x8
- Dec 9–Dec 15: TB=3x7, CL=3x11, AL=3x11
- Dec 16–Dec 22: TB=3x4, CL=3x8, AL=3x8
- Dec 23–Dec 29: TB=3x7, CL=3x11, AL=3x11
- Dec 30–Jan 5: TB=3x4, CL=3x8, AL=3x8

	Week 1 FRI	Week 2 MON	Week 3 FRI	Week 4 MON	Week 5 FRI	Week 6 MON
TOTAL BODY Squat Clean (FLR) TB WT Lifted	3x4 ___	3x7 ___	3x4 ___	3x7 ___	3x4 ___	3x7 ___
CHEST Bench Press CL WT Lifted	3x8 ___	3x11 ___	3x8 ___	3x11 ___	3x8 ___	3x11 ___
DB Flyes CL WT Lifted	3x8 ___	3x11 ___	3x8 ___	3x11 ___	3x8 ___	3x11 ___
TRUNK WT ALT V-Up WT Lifted	3x20 ___	3x20 ___	3x20 ___	3x20 ___	3x20 ___	3x20 ___
WT Seated Twist WT Lifted	3x20 ___	3x20 ___	3x20 ___	3x20 ___	3x20 ___	3x20 ___
UPPER BACK Seated Row/PD/T-Bar CL WT Lifted	3x8 ___	3x11 ___	3x8 ___	3x11 ___	3x8 ___	3x11 ___
NECK MR Lateral Flexion Reps Completed	2x8 ___	2x8 ___	2x8 ___	2x8 ___	2x8 ___	2x8 ___
ROTATOR CUFF Empty Cans Reps Completed	2x12 ___	2x12 ___	2x12 ___	2x12 ___	2x12 ___	2x12 ___
External Rotation Reps Completed	2x12 ___	2x12 ___	2x12 ___	2x12 ___	2x12 ___	2x12 ___

Friday/Monday Workout Regimen

Introduction Cycle

RUNNING BACKS/WIDE RECEIVERS

Monday
DATES: Jan 6–Jan 12
CYCLE: Introduction
GOAL: Reintroduce athletes to the demands of resistance training and emphasize correct technique.
LENGTH: 1 week
INTENSITY: Select a resistance that allows for completion of the full number of required repetitions on *each* set prior to increasing resistance.
PACE: Perform total-body lifts explosively. For all other exercises, lift in 2 seconds and lower in 4 seconds.
REST: 2:00 between sets and exercises
SETS/REPS:
- Jan 6–Jan 12: TB=3x5, CL=3x8, AL=3x8

	Week 1
TOTAL BODY Push Press TB WT Lifted	3x7 ____
LOWER BODY Squats CL WT Lifted	3x11 ____
Lunges CL (Total) WT Lifted	3x11 ____
TRUNK WT Crunch WT Lifted	3x20 ____
WT Twist Crunch WT Lifted	3x20 ____
WT Back Extensions WT Lifted	3x15 ____
UPPER BACK Seated Row/PD/T-Bar CL WT Lifted	3x11 ____
NECK MR Lateral Flexion Reps Completed	2x8 ____

Monday Workout Regimen

Wednesday

DATES: Jan 6–Jan 12
CYCLE: Introduction
GOAL: Reintroduce athletes to the demands of resistance training and emphasize correct technique.
LENGTH: 1 week
INTENSITY: Select a resistance that allows for completion of the full number of required repetitions on *each* set prior to increasing resistance.
PACE: Perform total-body lifts explosively. For all other exercises, lift in 2 seconds and lower in 4 seconds.
REST: 2:00 between sets and exercises
SETS/REPS:
- Jan 6–Jan 12: TB=3x7, CL=3x11, AL=3x11

	Week 1
TOTAL BODY DB Squat Clean (Shin) TB WT Lifted	3x7 ____
LOWER BODY DB Squats CL WT Lifted	3x11 ____
Leg Curl/MR Leg Curl AL WT Lifted	3x8/2x8 ____
TRUNK WT Toe Touch WT Lifted	3x20 ____
WT Twist Back Extension WT Lifted	3x15 ____
CHEST/SHOULDER DB Bench Press CL WT Lifted	3x11 ____
DB Front Raise CL WT Lifted	3x11 ____
DB Lateral Raise AL WT Lifted	3x11 ____

Wednesday Workout Regimen

Friday

DATES: Jan 6–Jan 12
CYCLE: Introduction
GOAL: Reintroduce athletes to the demands of resistance training and emphasize correct technique.
LENGTH: 1 week
INTENSITY: Select a resistance that allows for completion of the full number of required repetitions on *each* set prior to increasing resistance.
PACE: Perform total-body lifts explosively. For all other exercises, lift in 2 seconds and lower in 4 seconds.
REST: 2:00 between sets and exercises
SETS/REPS:
- Jan 6–Jan 12: TB=3x5, CL=3x8, AL=3x8

	Week 1
TOTAL BODY Squat Clean (FLR) WT Lifted	3x5 ____
CHEST Bench Press CL WT Lifted	3x8 ____
DB Flyes AL WT Lifted	3x8 ____
TRUNK WT V-Up WT Lifted	3x20 ____
WT Seated Twist WT Lifted	3x20 ____
UPPER BACK Seated Row/PD/T-Bar CL WT Lifted	3x8 ____
BICEPS Any Biceps Exercise AL WT Lifted	3x8 ____
NECK MR Flexion/Extension Reps Completed	2x8 ____

Friday Workout Regimen

Strength Cycle I

DEFENSIVE BACKS

Monday/Friday
DATES: Jan 13–Feb 9
CYCLE: Strength I
GOAL: Increase muscle strength, because of the positive relationship between muscle strength and power.
LENGTH: 4 weeks
INTENSITY: Select a resistance that allows for completion of the full number of required repetitions on each set prior to increasing resistance.
PACE: Perform total-body lifts explosively. For all other exercises, lift in 2 seconds and lower in 3 seconds.
REST: 2:00 between all sets and exercises
SETS/REPS:

- Jan 13–Jan 19: TB=3x6, CL=3x9, AL=3x9
- Jan 20–Jan 26: TB=4x4, CL=4x7, AL=3x7
- Jan 27–Feb 2: TB=4x6, CL=4x9, AL=3x9
- Feb 3–Feb 9: TB=4x4, CL=4x7, AL=3x7

	Week 1 MON	Week 2 FRI	Week 3 MON	Week 4 FRI
TOTAL BODY Split ALT FT Snatch (FLR) TB WT Lifted	3x6 ___	4x4 ___	4x6 ___	4x4 ___
LOWER BODY Squats CL WT Lifted	3x9 ___	4x7 ___	4x9 ___	4x7 ___
Bar/Keg/Log RDL CL WT Lifted (Perform 1 Set Keg/Log)	3x9 ___	3x7 ___	3x9 ___	3x7 ___
TRUNK WT Decline Crunch WT Lifted	3x20 ___	3x20 ___	3x20 ___	3x20 ___
WT Twist Glute Ham WT Lifted	3x10 ___	3x10 ___	3x10 ___	3x10 ___
UPPER BACK Seated Row/PD/T-Bar CL WT Lift	3x9 ___	4x7 ___	4x9 ___	4x7 ___
BICEPS Any Biceps Exercise AL WT Lift	3x9 ___	3x7 ___	3x9 ___	3x7 ___
NECK MR Flexion/Extension Reps Completed	2x8 ___	2x8 ___	2x8 ___	2x8 ___

Monday/Friday Workout Regimen

Wednesday
DATES: Jan 13–Feb 9
CYCLE: Strength I
GOAL: Increase muscle strength, because of the positive relationship between muscle strength and power.
LENGTH: 4 weeks
INTENSITY: Select a resistance that allows for completion of the full number of required repetitions on *each* set prior to increasing resistance.
PACE: Perform total-body lifts explosively. For all other exercises, lift in 2 seconds and lower in 3 seconds.
REST: 2:00 between all sets and exercises
SETS/REPS:
- Jan 13–Jan 19: TB=3x6, CL=3x9, AL=3x9
- Jan 20–Jan 26: TB=4x4, CL=4x7, AL=3x7
- Jan 27–Feb 2: TB=4x6, CL=4x9, AL=3x9
- Feb 3–Feb 9: TB=4x4, CL=4x7, AL=3x7

	Week 1	Week 2	Week 3	Week 4
TOTAL BODY DB/Tire Squat Clean (Shin) TB WT Lifted	3x6 ___	4x4 ___	4x6 ___	4x4 ___
LOWER BODY DB Squat CL WT Lifted	3x9 ___	4x7 ___	4x9 ___	4x7 ___
DB/Keg/Log SLDL WT Lifted (Perform 1 Set Keg/Log)	3x9 ___	3x7 ___	3x9 ___	3x7 ___
TRUNK WT Bicycles WT Lifted	3x20 ___	3x20 ___	3x20 ___	3x20 ___
WT Glute Ham WT Lifted	3x10 ___	3x10 ___	3x10 ___	3x10 ___
UPPER BODY DB/Keg/Log Bench CL WT Lifted (Perform 1 Set Keg/Log)	3x9 ___	4x7 ___	4x9 ___	4x7 ___
DB/Keg/Log Incline CL WT Lifted	3x9 ___	4x7 ___	4x9 ___	4x7 ___
DB Row CL WT Lifted	3x9 ___	4x7 ___	4x9 ___	4x7 ___

Wednesday Workout Regimen

Friday/Monday

DATES: Jan 13–Feb 9
CYCLE: Strength I
GOAL: Increase muscle strength, because of the positive relationship between muscle strength and power.
LENGTH: 4 weeks
INTENSITY: Select a resistance that allows for completion of the full number of required repetitions on *each* set prior to increasing resistance.
PACE: Perform total-body lifts explosively. For all other exercises, lift in 2 seconds and lower in 3 seconds.
REST: 2:00 between all sets and exercises
SETS/REPS:

- Jan 13–Jan 19: TB=3x4, CL=3x7, AL=3x9
- Jan 20–Jan 26: TB=4x6, CL=4x9, AL=3x7
- Jan 27–Feb 2: TB=4x4, CL=4x7, AL=3x9
- Feb 3–Feb 9: TB=4x6, CL=4x9, AL=3x7

	Week 1 FRI	Week 2 MON	Week 3 FRI	Week 4 MON
TOTAL BODY Squat Clean (FLR) TB WT Lifted	3x4 ____	4x6 ____	4x4 ____	4x6 ____
CHEST Bench Press CL WT Lifted	3x7 ____	4x9 ____	4x7 ____	4x9 ____
Log/Keg Incline Press CL WT Lifted	3x7 ____	4x9 ____	4x7 ____	4x9 ____
1x60-Second Stabilization Each Leg	1x60 sec ____	1x60 sec ____	1x60 sec ____	1x60 sec ____
MR Neck MR Lateral Flexion Reps Completed	2x8 ____	2x8 ____	2x8 ____	2x8 ____
MR Training (Prepare for maximum effort in the gym)	See Board	See Board	See Board	See Board

Friday/Monday Workout Regimen

Strength Cycle II

KICKERS

Monday/Friday
DATES: Feb 10–March 23
CYCLE: Strength II
GOAL: Increase muscle strength, because of the positive relationship between strength and power.
LENGTH: 6 weeks
INTENSITY: Select a resistance that allows for completion of the full number of required repetitions on the *first* set only prior to increasing resistance.
PACE: Perform total-body lifts explosively. For all other exercises, lift in 2 seconds and lower in 3 seconds.
REST: 2:30 between total-body exercises, 2:00 between all other sets and exercises
SETS/REPS:

- Feb 10–Feb 16: TB=4x5, CL=4x6, AL=3x6
- Feb 17–Feb 23: TB=4x3, CL=4x4, AL=3x6
- Feb 24–March 2: TB=4x5, CL=4x6, AL=3x6
- March 3–March 9: TB=4x3, CL=4x4, AL=3x6
- March 10–March 16: TB=4x5, CL=4x6, AL=3x6
- March 17–March 23: TB=4x3, CL=4x4, AL=3x6

	Week 1 MON	Week 2 FRI	Week 3 MON	Week 4 FRI	Week 5 MON	Week 6 FRI
TOTAL BODY Squat Clean (FLR) TB WT Lifted	4x5 ___	4x3 ___	4x5 ___	4x3 ___	4x5 ___	4x3 ___
Split Snatch Balance TB WT Lifted	4x5 ___	4x3 ___	4x5 ___	4x3 ___	4x5 ___	4x3 ___
CHEST Bench CL (Partial First Set) WT Lifted	4x6 ___	4x4 ___	4x6 ___	4x4 ___	4x6 ___	4x4 ___
TRUNK MB Decline 1-Arm Throw WT Lifted	3x15 ___	3x15 ___	3x15 ___	3x15 ___	3x15 ___	3x15 ___
WT Reverse Back Extension WT Lifted	3x10 ___	3x10 ___	3x10 ___	3x10 ___	3x10 ___	3x10 ___
UPPER BACK Seated Row/PD/T-Bar Row CL WT Lifted	4x6 ___	4x4 ___	4x6 ___	4x4 ___	4x6 ___	4x4 ___
NECK MR Flexion/Extension Reps Completed	2x8 ___	2x8 ___	2x8 ___	2x8 ___	2x8 ___	2x8 ___
MR Lateral Flexion Reps Completed	2x8 ___	2x8 ___	2x8 ___	2x8 ___	2x8 ___	2x8 ___

Monday/Friday Workout Regimen

Wednesday

DATES: Feb 10–March 23
CYCLE: Strength II
GOAL: Increase muscle strength, because of the positive relationship between strength and power.
LENGTH: 6 weeks
INTENSITY: Select a resistance that allows for completion of the full number of required repetitions on the *first* set only prior to increasing resistance.
PACE: Perform total-body lifts explosively. For all other exercises, lift in 2 seconds and lower in 3 seconds.
REST: 2:30 between total-body exercises, 2:00 between all other sets and exercises
SETS/REPS:

- Feb 10–Feb 16: TB=4x3, CL=4x4, AL=3x6
- Feb 17–Feb 23: TB=4x5, CL=4x6, AL=3x6
- Feb 24–March 2: TB=4x3, CL=4x4, AL=3x6
- March 3–March 9: TB=4x5, CL=4x6, AL=3x6
- March 10–March 16: TB=4x3, CL=4x4, AL=3x6
- March 17–March 23: TB=4x5, CL=4x6, AL=3x6

	Week 1	Week 2	Week 3	Week 4	Week 5	Week 6
TOTAL BODY DB Split ALT FT Snatch TB (Shin) WT Lifted	4x3 ___	4x5 ___	4x3 ___	4x5 ___	4x3 ___	4x5 ___
LOWER BODY DB/Keg/Log 1-Leg Squat CL WT Lifted (Partial First Set) (Perform 1 Set Keg/Log)	4x4 ___	4x6 ___	4x4 ___	4x6 ___	4x4 ___	4x6 ___
Hip Flexion CL WT Lifted	3x6 ___	3x6 ___	3x6 ___	3x6 ___	3x6 ___	3x6 ___
Leg Curl/MR Leg Curl AL WT Lifted	3x6/2x8 ___	3x6/2x8 ___	3x6/2x8 ___	3x6/2x8 ___	3x6/2x8 ___	3x6/2x8 ___
Leg Drive Reps Completed	1x5 ___	1x5 ___	1x5 ___	1x5 ___	1x5 ___	1x5 ___
TRUNK MB Circles Reps Completed	3x15 ___	3x15 ___	3x15 ___	3x15 ___	3x15 ___	3x15 ___
WT Decline Crunch WT Lifted	3x15 ___	3x15 ___	3x15 ___	3x15 ___	3x15 ___	3x15 ___
CHEST DB/Keg/Log Incline CL WT Lifted (Partial First Set) (Perform 1 Set Keg/Log)	4x4 ___	4x6 ___	4x4 ___	4x6 ___	4x4 ___	4x6 ___
SHOULDERS MR Upright Row Reps (1-Leg/Eyes Closed)	2x8 ___	2x8 ___	2x8 ___	2x8 ___	2x8 ___	2x8 ___

Wednesday Workout Regimen

Friday/Monday

DATES: Feb 10–March 23
CYCLE: Strength II
GOAL: Increase muscle strength, because of the positive relationship between strength and power.
LENGTH: 6 weeks
INTENSITY: Select a resistance that allows for completion of the full number of required repetitions on the *first* set only prior to increasing resistance.
PACE: Perform total-body lifts explosively. For all other exercises, lift in 2 seconds and lower in 3 seconds.
REST: 2:30 between total-body exercises, 2:00 between all other sets and exercises
SETS/REPS:

- Feb 10–Feb 16: TB=4x3, CL=4x4, AL=3x6
- Feb 17–Feb 23: TB=4x5, CL=4x6, AL=3x6
- Feb 24–March 2: TB=4x3, CL=4x4, AL=3x6
- March 3–March 9: TB=4x5, CL=4x6, AL=3x6
- March 10–March 16: TB=4x3, CL=4x4, AL=3x6
- March 17–March 23: TB=4x5, CL=4x6, AL=3x6

	Week 1 FRI	Week 2 MON	Week 3 FRI	Week 4 MON	Week 5 FRI	Week 6 MON
TOTAL BODY Split ALT FT Snatch (FLR) TB WT Lifted	4x3 ___	4x5 ___	4x3 ___	4x5 ___	4x3 ___	4x5 ___
LOWER BODY Squats CL (Partial First Set) WT Lifted	4x4 ___	4x6 ___	4x4 ___	4x6 ___	4x4 ___	4x6 ___
Leg Extension AL WT Lifted	3x7 ___	3x7 ___	3x7 ___	3x7 ___	3x7 ___	3x7 ___
1x60-Second Stabilization Each Leg	1x60 sec ___	1x60 sec ___	1x60 sec ___	1x60 sec ___	1x60 sec ___	1x60 sec ___
TRUNK Hang Straight-Leg Lifts WT Lifted	3x15 ___	3x15 ___	3x15 ___	3x15 ___	3x15 ___	3x15 ___
Decline Leg Throws Reps Completed	3x15 ___	3x15 ___	3x15 ___	3x15 ___	3x15 ___	3x15 ___
WT Reverse Back Extension WT Lifted	3x10 ___	3x10 ___	3x10 ___	3x10 ___	3x10 ___	3x10 ___
UPPER BACK MR Seated Row WT Lifted	2x8 ___	2x8 ___	2x8 ___	2x8 ___	2x8 ___	2x8 ___

Friday/Monday Workout Regimen

Strength Cycle III

QUARTERBACKS

Monday/Friday
DATES: April 28–May 18
CYCLE: Strength III
GOAL: Increase muscle strength, because of the positive relationship between strength and power.
LENGTH: 3 weeks
INTENSITY: Select a resistance that allows for completion of the full number of required repetitions on the *first* set only prior to increasing resistance.
PACE: Perform total-body lifts explosively. For all other exercises, lift in 2 seconds and lower in 3 seconds.
REST: 2:30 between total-body exercises, 2:00 between all other sets and exercises
SETS/REPS:

- April 28–May 5: TB=4x4, CL=4x5, AL=3x6
- May 6–May 12: TB=4x3, CL=4x3, AL=3x6
- May 13–May 18: TB=4x3, CL=4x3, AL=3x6

	Week 1 MON	Week 2 FRI	Week 3 MON
TOTAL BODY			
Split ALT FT Snatch TB (FLR) WT Lifted	4x4 ____	4x3 ____	4x3 ____
Split ALT FT Jerk TB WT Lifted	4x4 ____	4x3 ____	4x3 ____
LOWER BODY			
Squats (Partial First Set) CL WT Lifted	4x5 ____	4x3 ____	4x3 ____
Lunge/Keg/Log CL WT Lifted (Total)	4x5 ____	4x3 ____	4x3 ____
60-Second Stabilization Each Leg	1x60 sec ____	1x60 sec ____	1x60 sec ____
Leg Drive Reps Completed	1x5 ____	1x5 ____	1x5 ____
TRUNK			
WT ALT V-Ups/with MB Reps Completed	3x12 ____	3x12 ____	3x12 ____
WT Reverse Back Extension WT Lifted	3x10 ____	3x10 ____	3x10 ____
UPPER BACK			
Seated Row/Pull-Down/T-Bar CL WT Lifted	4x5 ____	4x3 ____	4x3 ____
ROTATOR CUFF			
Empty Cans Reps Completed	2x10 ____	2x10 ____	2x10 ____
NECK			
MR Flexion/Extension Reps Completed	2x8 ____	2x8 ____	2x8 ____

Monday/Friday Workout Regimen

Wednesday

DATES: April 28–May 18
CYCLE: Strength III
GOAL: Increase muscle strength, because of the positive relationship between strength and power.
LENGTH: 3 weeks
INTENSITY: Select a resistance that allows for completion of the full number of required repetitions on the *first* set only prior to increasing resistance.
PACE: Perform total-body lifts explosively. For all other exercises, lift in 2 seconds and lower in 3 seconds.
REST: 2:30 between total-body exercises, 2:00 between all other sets and exercises
SETS/REPS:

- April 28–May 5: TB=4x3, CL=4x3, AL=3x8
- May 6–May 12: TB=4x4, CL=4x5, AL=3x8
- May 13–May 18: TB=4x3, CL=4x3, AL=3x8

	Week 1	Week 2	Week 3
TOTAL BODY DB Hang Split ALT FT Snatch TB WT Lifted	4x3 ___	4x4 ___	4x3 ___
LOWER BODY DB/Keg 1-Leg Squat CL WT Lifted (Partial First Set)	4x3 ___	4x5 ___	4x3 ___
DB/Keg Log Lateral Squat CL WT Lifted (Total)	4x3 ___	4x5 ___	4x3 ___
Leg Curls/MR Leg Curls AL WT Lifted	3x6/2x8 ___	3x6/2x8 ___	3x6/2x8 ___
TRUNK MB Push-Downs Reps Completed	3x12 ___	3x12 ___	3x12 ___
MB Twist Push-Downs Reps Completed	3x12 ___	3x12 ___	3x12 ___
CHEST DB/Keg/Log Incline Press CL WT Lifted (Partial First Set)	4x3 ___	4x5 ___	4x3 ___
ARMS MR Standing Triceps Reps Completed (1-Leg/Eyes Closed)	2x8 ___	2x8 ___	2x8 ___

Wednesday Workout Regimen

Friday/Monday

DATES: April 28–May 18
CYCLE: Strength III
GOAL: Increase muscle strength, because of the positive relationship between strength and power.
LENGTH: 3 weeks
INTENSITY: Select a resistance that allows for completion of the full number of required repetitions on the *first* set only prior to increasing resistance.
PACE: Perform total-body lifts explosively. For all other exercises, lift in 2 seconds and lower in 3 seconds.
REST: 2:30 between total-body exercises, 2:00 between all other sets and exercises
SETS/REPS:

- April 28–May 5: TB=4x3, CL=4x3, AL=3x6
- May 6–May 12: TB=4x4, CL=4x5, AL=3x6
- May 13–May 18: TB=4x3, CL=4x3, AL=3x6

	Week 1 FRI	Week 2 MON	Week 3 FRI
TOTAL BODY Squat Cleans TB (FLR) WT Lifted	4x3 ___	4x4 ___	4x3 ___
Split ALT FT Snatch Balance TB WT Lifted	4x3 ___	4x4 ___	4x3 ___
CHEST Bench Press (Perform 1 Set Standing) WT Lifted (Partial First Set)	4x3 ___	4x5 ___	4x3 ___
TRUNK MB Decline 1-Arm Throws Reps Completed	3x12 ___	3x12 ___	3x12 ___
WT Reverse Back Extension WT Lifted	3x10 ___	3x10 ___	3x10 ___
SHOULDERS MR Front Raise (1-Leg/Eyes Closed) Reps Completed	2x8 ___	2x8 ___	2x8 ___
ROTATOR CUFF Internal Rotations Reps Completed	2x10 ___	2x10 ___	2x10 ___
NECK MR Lateral Flexion Reps Completed	2x8 ___	2x8 ___	2x8 ___

Friday/Monday Workout Regimen

Strength Cycle IV

RUNNING BACK/WIDE RECEIVER

Monday/Friday
DATES: May 19–June 8
CYCLE: Strength IV
GOAL: Increase muscle strength, because of the positive relationship between strength and power.
LENGTH: 3 weeks
INTENSITY: Select a resistance that allows for completion of the full number of required repetitions on the *first* set only prior to increasing resistance.
PACE: Perform total-body lifts explosively. For all other exercises, lower in 2 seconds and lift as explosively as possible.
REST: 2:30 between total-body exercises, 2:00 between all other sets and exercises
SETS/REPS:
- May 19–May 25: TB=4x4, CL=4x4, AL=3x6
- May 26–June 1: TB=4x2, CL=4x2, AL=3x6
- June 2–June 8: TB=4x4, CL=4x4, AL=3x6

	Week 1 MON	Week 2 FRI	Week 3 MON
TOTAL BODY Hang Squat Clean TB WT Lifted	4x4 ___	4x2 ___	4x4 ___
Split ALT FT Jerk TB WT Lifted	4x4 ___	4x2 ___	4x4 ___
CHEST Bench CL (Perform 1 Set Standing) WT Lifted (Partial First Set)	4x4 ___	4x2 ___	4x4 ___
TRUNK MB Forward Stand Twist Throw WT Lifted	3x10 ___	3x10 ___	3x10 ___
MB Decline 1-Arm Throw WT Lifted	3x8 ___	3x8 ___	3x8 ___
SHOULDERS MR Lateral Raise Reps (1-Leg/Eyes Closed)	2x8 ___	2x8 ___	2x8 ___
UPPER BACK Keg Bent Row AL Reps Completed	3x6 ___	3x6 ___	3x6 ___
NECK MR Flexion/Extension Reps Completed	2x8 ___	2x8 ___	2x8 ___

Monday/Friday Workout Regimen

Wednesday

DATES: May 19–June 8
CYCLE: Strength IV
GOAL: Increase muscle strength, because of the positive relationship between strength and power.
LENGTH: 3 weeks
INTENSITY: Select a resistance that allows for completion of the full number of required repetitions on the *first* set only prior to increasing resistance.
PACE: Perform total-body lifts explosively. For all other exercises, lower in 2 seconds and lift as explosively as possible.
REST: 2:30 between total-body exercises, 2:00 between all other sets and exercises
SETS/REPS:

- May 19–May 25: TB=4x4, CL=4x4, AL=3x6
- May 26–June 1: TB=4x2, CL=4x2, AL=3x6
- June 2–June 8: TB=4x4, CL=4x4, AL=3x6

	Week 1	Week 2	Week 3
TOTAL BODY DB/Tire Hang Squat ALT Clean TB WT Lifted	4x4 ____	4x2 ____	4x4 ____
DB Split ALT FT ALT Jerk TB WT Lifted	4x4 ____	4x2 ____	4x4 ____
LOWER BODY DB/Keg 1-Leg Front Squat CL WT Lifted (Each Leg)	4x4 ____	4x2 ____	4x4 ____
DB/Keg/Log Side Lunge CL WT Lifted (Total)	4x4 ____	4x2 ____	4x4 ____
TRUNK MB Stand 1-Leg ALT Reverse Crunch Reps Completed	3x10 ____	3x10 ____	3x10 ____
Twist Keg Lift WT Lifted	3x8 ____	3x8 ____	3x8 ____
CHEST DB/Keg/Log ALT Incline (Partial First Set) CL WT Lifted (Total)	4x4 ____	4x2 ____	4x4 ____
ARMS MR ALT Biceps (1-Leg/Eyes Closed) Reps Completed (Each Arm)	2x8 ____	2x8 ____	2x8 ____

Wednesday Workout Regimen

Friday/Monday

DATES: May 19–June 8
CYCLE: Strength IV
GOAL: Increase muscle strength, because of the positive relationship between strength and power.
LENGTH: 3 weeks
INTENSITY: Select a resistance that allows for completion of the full number of required repetitions on the *first* set only prior to increasing resistance.
PACE: Perform total-body lifts explosively. For all other exercises, lower in 2 seconds and lift as explosively as possible.
REST: 2:30 between total-body exercises, 2:00 between all other sets and exercises
SETS/REPS:
- May 19–May 25: TB=4x2, CL=4x2, AL=3x6
- May 26–June 1: TB=4x4, CL=4x4, AL=3x6
- June 2–June 8: TB=4x2, CL=4x2, AL=3x6

	Week 1 MON	Week 2 FRI	Week 3 MON
TOTAL BODY			
Hang Split ALT FT Snatch TB WT Lifted	4x2 ___	4x4 ___	4x2 ___
Spilt ALT FT Jerk TB WT Lifted	4x2 ___	4x4 ___	4x2 ___
LOWER BODY			
Squats (Partial First Set) CL WT Lift	4x2 ___	4x4 ___	4x2 ___
DB/Keg/Log 1-Leg SLDL CL WT Lifted (Each Leg)	3x6 ___	3x6 ___	3x6 ___
1x60-Second Stabilization Each Leg	1x60 sec ___	1x60 sec ___	1x60 sec ___
Leg Drive Reps Completed	1x5 ___	1x5 ___	1x5 ___
TRUNK			
Sit Fit 1-Leg Wood Chop Reps Completed	3x10 ___	3x10 ___	3x10 ___
WT Twist 1-Leg Glute Ham WT Lifted	3x8 ___	3x8 ___	3x8 ___
UPPER BACK			
Pull-Down/Seated Row/T-Bar CL WT Lifted	4x2 ___	4x4 ___	4x2 ___
NECK			
MR Lateral Flexion Reps Completed	2x8 ___	2x8 ___	2x8 ___

Friday/Monday Workout Regimen

Power Cycle I

DEFENSIVE BACKS

Monday/Friday

DATES: June 9–July 6
CYCLE: Power I
GOAL: Increase muscle power, because of the positive relationship between muscle power and performance.
LENGTH: 4 weeks
INTENSITY: On total-body exercises, select a resistance that allows for completion of the full number of required repetitions on the *first* set only prior to increasing resistance. On timed exercises, reduce the resistance as necessary to maintain the desired speed of movement during each set.
PACE: Perform total-body lifts explosively. Perform timed lifts at a pace that allows for completion of the required number of repetitions in the specified time period.
REST: 3:00 between total-body exercises, 2:30 between all other sets and exercises
SETS/REPS:
- June 9–June 15: TB=5x3, TL=4x5@8 sec (1.5)
- June 16–June 22: TB=5x2, TL=4x3@4 sec (1.2)
- June 23–June 29: TB=5x3, TL=4x5@8 sec (1.5)
- June 30–July 6: TB=5x2, TL=4x3@4 sec (1.2)

	Week 1 MON	Week 2 FRI	Week 3 MON	Week 4 FRI
TOTAL BODY Hang Split ALT FT Snatch TB WT Lifted (On Command)	5x3 ___	5x2 ___	5x3 ___	5x2 ___
Split ALT FT Jerk TB WT Lifted	5x3 ___	5x2@85% ___	5x3@75% ___	5x2@85% ___
LOWER BODY Squats CL WT Lifted	1x5 ___	1x3 ___	1x5 ___	1x3 ___
Squats TL WT Lifted	3x5@8 sec ___	3x3@4 sec ___	3x5@8 sec ___	3x3@4 sec ___
Keg/Log Pivot Lunges TL WT Lifted (Total)	4x5@8 sec ___	4x3@4 sec ___	4x5@8 sec ___	4x3@4 sec ___
1x60-Second Stabilization Each Leg	1x60 sec	1x60 sec	1x60 sec	1x60 sec
Leg Drive Reps Completed	1x5 ___	1x5 ___	1x5 ___	1x5 ___
TRUNK MB Off-Center Rotate Throw WT Lifted	3x10 ___	3x10 ___	3x10 ___	3x10 ___
Sit Fit 1-Leg Chop Throws WT Lifted	3x10 ___	3x10 ___	3x10 ___	3x10 ___
UPPER BACK MR Upright Row Reps (1-Leg/Eyes Closed)	2x8 ___	2x8 ___	2x8 ___	2x8 ___
NECK MR Flexion/Extension Reps Completed	2x8 ___	2x8 ___	2x8 ___	2x8 ___

Monday/Friday Workout Regimen

Wednesday

DATES: June 9–July 6
CYCLE: Power I
GOAL: Increase muscle power, because of the positive relationship between muscle power and performance.
LENGTH: 4 weeks
INTENSITY: On total-body exercises, select a resistance that allows for completion of the full number of required repetitions on the *first* set only prior to increasing resistance. On timed exercises, reduce the resistance as necessary to maintain the desired speed of movement during each set.
PACE: Perform total-body lifts explosively. Perform timed lifts at a pace that allows for completion of the required number of repetitions in the specified time period.
REST: 3:00 between total-body exercises, 2:30 between all other sets and exercises
SETS/REPS:

- June 9–June 15: TB=5x3, TL=4x5@8 sec (1.5)
- June 16–June 22: TB=5x2, TL=4x3@4 sec (1.2)
- June 23–June 29: TB=5x3, TL=4x5@8 sec (1.5)
- June 30–July 6: TB=5x2, TL=4x3@4 sec (1.2)

	Week 1	Week 2	Week 3	Week 4
TOTAL BODY				
DB Hang Split ALT FT ALT Snatch TB WT Lifted (On Command)	5x3 ____	5x2 ____	5x3 ____	5x2 ____
DB Split ALT FT ALT Jerk TB WT Lifted	5x3 ____	5x2@85% ____	5x3@75% ____	5x2@85% ____
LOWER BODY				
DB/Keg/Log Jump Lunge TL WT Lifted (Total)	4x5@8 sec ____	4x3@4 sec ____	4x5@8 sec ____	4x3@4 sec ____
DB Lateral Step-Up/Crossover Off WT Lifted (Total)	4x6 ____	4x3 ____	4x6 ____	4x3 ____
Leg Curl TL WT Lifted	4x6@9 sec ____	4x3@4 sec ____	4x6@9 sec ____	4x3@4 sec ____
TRUNK				
MB Forward Stand Twist Throw WT Lifted	3x10 ____	3x10 ____	3x10 ____	3x10 ____
WT Reverse Back Extension 3x8 WT Lifted	3x8 ____	3x8 ____	3x8 ____	____
CHEST				
DB/Keg/Log Incline Press TL WT Lifted (Total)	4x5@8 sec ____	4x3@4 sec ____	4x5@8 sec ____	4x3@4 sec ____
ARMS				
DB ALT Biceps AL WT Lifted (Each Arm)	3x6 ____	3x6 ____	3x6 ____	3x6 ____

Wednesday Workout Regimen

Friday/Monday

DATES: June 9–July 6

CYCLE: Power I

GOAL: Increase muscle power, because of the positive relationship between muscle power and performance.

LENGTH: 4 weeks

INTENSITY: On total-body exercises, select a resistance that allows for completion of the full number of required repetitions on the *first* set only prior to increasing resistance. On timed exercises, reduce the resistance as necessary to maintain the desired speed of movement during each set.

PACE: Perform total-body lifts explosively. Perform timed lifts at a pace that allows for completion of the required number of repetitions in the specified time period.

REST: 3:00 between total-body exercises, 2:30 between all other sets and exercises

SETS/REPS:

- June 9–June 15: TB=5x2, TL=4x3@4 sec (1.2)
- June 16–June 22: TB=5x3, TL=4x5@8 sec (1.5)
- June 23–June 29: TB=5x2, TL=4x3@4 sec (1.2)
- June 30–July 6: TB=5x3, TL=4x5@8 sec (1.5)

	Week 1 FRI	Week 2 MON	Week 3 FRI	Week 4 MON
TOTAL BODY Hang Squat Clean TB WT Lifted	5x2 ___	5x3 ___	5x2 ___	5x3 ___
Split ALT FT Snatch Balance TB WT Lifted	5x2 ___	5x3@75% ___	5x2@85% ___	5x3@75% ___
CHEST Bench CL (Perform 1 Set Standing) WT Lifted	1x3 ___	1x5 ___	1x3 ___	1x5 ___
Bench Press TL WT Lifted	3x3@4 sec ___	3x5@8 sec ___	3x3@4 sec ___	3x5@8 sec ___
TRUNK MB Decline 2-Ball Twist Reps Completed	3x10 ___	3x10 ___	3x10 ___	3x10 ___
Sit Fit 1-Leg MB Chop/Twist Reps Completed	3x10 ___	3x10 ___	3x10 ___	3x10 ___
WT Reverse Back Extension WT Lifted	3x8 ___	3x8 ___	3x8 ___	3x8 ___
UPPER BACK Towel Grip Seated Row WT Lifted	4x3@4 sec ___	4x5@8 sec ___	4x3@4 sec ___	4x5@8 sec ___
NECK MR Lateral Flexion Reps Completed	2x8 ___	2x8 ___	2x8 ___	2x8 ___

Friday/Monday Workout Regimen

Power Cycle II

KICKERS

Monday/Friday
DATES: July 7–July 27
CYCLE: Power II
GOAL: Further increase muscle power, because of the positive relationship between muscle power and performance.
LENGTH: 3 weeks
INTENSITY: On total-body exercises, select a resistance that allows for completion of the full number of required repetitions on the *first* set only prior to increasing resistance. On timed exercises, reduce the resistance as necessary to maintain the desired speed of movement each set.
PACE: Perform total-body lifts explosively. Perform timed lifts at a pace that allows for completion of the required number of repetitions in the specified time period. For all other exercises, lift in 2 seconds and lower in 3 seconds.
REST: 3:00 between total-body exercises, 2:30 between all other sets and exercises
SETS/REPS:
- July 7–July 13: TB=4x3, TL=4x4@3 sec (.8)
- July 14–July 20: TB=4x2, TL=4x2@2 sec (1)
- July 21–July 27: TB=4x1, TL=4x2@2 sec (1)

	Week 1 MON	Week 2 FRI	Week 3 MON
TOTAL BODY Hang Squat Clean TB WT Lifted	4x3 ___	4x2 ___	4x1 ___
Split ALT FT Snatch Balance TB WT Lifted	4x3 ___	4x2@60% ___	4x1@50% ___
CHEST Bench (Perform 1 Set Standing) CL WT Lifted	1x4 ___	1x2 ___	1x2 ___
Bench Press TL WT Lifted	3x4@3 sec ___	3x2@2 sec ___	3x2@2 sec ___
TRUNK Standing MR Twists WT Lifted	3x10 ___	3x10 ___	3x10 ___
Decline Leg Throws WT Lifted	3x10 ___	3x10 ___	3x10 ___
UPPER BACK MR Upright Row Reps Completed (1-Leg/Eyes Closed)	2x8 ___	2x8 ___	2x8 ___
NECK MR Lateral Flexion Reps Completed	2x8 ___	2x8 ___	2x8 ___

Monday/Friday Workout Regimen

Wednesday

DATES: July 7–July 27
CYCLE: Power II
GOAL: Further increase muscle power, because of the positive relationship between muscle power and performance.
LENGTH: 3 weeks
INTENSITY: On total-body exercises, select a resistance that allows for completion of the full number of required repetitions on the *first* set only prior to increasing resistance. On timed exercises, reduce the resistance as necessary to maintain the desired speed of movement during each set.
PACE: Perform total-body lifts explosively. Perform timed lifts at a pace that allows for completion of the required number of repetitions in the specified time period. For all other exercises, lift in 2 seconds and lower in 3 seconds.
REST: 3:00 between total-body exercises, 2:30 between all other sets and exercises
SETS/REPS:

- July 7–July 13: TB=4x3, TL=4x4@3 sec (.8)
- July 14–July 20: TB=4x2, TL=4x2@2 sec (1)
- July 21–July 27: TB=4x1, TL=4x2@2 sec (1)

	Week 1	Week 2	Week 3
TOTAL BODY DB/Tire Squat Hang ALT Cleans TB WT Lifted	4x3 ___	4x2 ___	4x1 ___
DB Split ALT FT ALT Jerks TB WT Lifted	4x3 ___	4x2@60% ___	4x1@50% ___
LOWER BODY DB/Keg/Log 1-Leg Front Squat TL WT Lifted (Each Leg)	4x4@3 sec ___	4x2@2 sec ___	4x2@2 sec ___
Leg Extensions TL WT Lifted	4x4@3 sec ___	4x2@2 sec ___	4x2@2 sec ___
MR Leg Curls Reps Completed	2x8 ___	2x8 ___	2x8 ___
TRUNK 1-Leg Wood Chop/Twist WT Lifted	3x10 ___	3x10 ___	3x10 ___
WT Twist 1-Leg Back Extension WT Lifted	3x8 ___	3x8 ___	3x8 ___
CHEST DB/Keg/Log ALT Bench TL WT Lifted (Total)	4x4@3 sec ___	4x2@2 sec ___	4x2@2 sec ___
NECK MR Flexion/Extension Reps Completed	2x8 ___	2x8 ___	2x8 ___

Wednesday Workout Regimen

Friday/Monday

DATES: July 7–July 27
CYCLE: Power II
GOAL: Further increase muscle power, because of the positive relationship between muscle power and performance.
LENGTH: 3 weeks
INTENSITY: On total-body exercises, select a resistance that allows for completion of the full number of required repetitions on the *first* set only prior to increasing resistance. On timed exercises, reduce the resistance as necessary to maintain the desired speed of movement during each set.
PACE: Perform total-body lifts explosively. Perform timed lifts at a pace that allows for completion of the required number of repetitions in the specified time period. For all other exercises, lift in 2 seconds and lower in 3 seconds.
REST: 3:00 between total-body exercises, 2:30 between all other sets and exercises
SETS/REPS:

- July 7–July 13: TB=4x3, TL=4x4@3 sec (.8)
- July 14–July 20: TB=4x2, TL=4x2@2 sec (1)
- July 21–July 27: TB=4x1, TL=4x2@2 sec (1)

	Week 1 FRI	Week 2 MON	Week 3 FRI
TOTAL BODY			
Hang Split ALT FT Snatch TB WT Lifted (On Command)	4x3 ____	4x2 ____	4x1 ____
Split ALT FT Jerks TB WT Lifted	4x3 ____	4x2@60% ____	4x2@50% ____
CHEST			
Squats CL WT Lifted	1x4 ____	1x2 ____	1x2 ____
Squats TL WT Lifted	3x4@3 sec ____	3x2@2 sec ____	3x2@2 sec ____
Hip Flexion TL WT Lifted	4x4@3 sec ____	4x2@2 sec ____	4x2@2 sec ____
60-Second Stabilization Reps Completed (Each Leg)	1x60 sec	1x60 sec	1x60 sec
Leg Drive Reps Completed	1x5 ____	1x5 ____	1x5 ____
TRUNK			
Hanging Leg Throws WT Lifted	3x10 ____	3x10 ____	3x10 ____
WT 1-Leg Back Extensions WT Lifted	3x8 ____	3x8 ____	3x8 ____
UPPER BACK			
Seated Row/PD/T-Bar Row CL Reps Comp (1-Leg/Eyes Closed)	4x4@3 sec ____	4x2@2 sec ____	4x2@2 sec ____

Friday/Monday Workout Regimen

In-Season Cycle I

QUARTERBACKS

Day 1
Note that the in-season workouts are labeled with Day 1 and Day 2 rather than with a specific day. Because the competition schedule varies (for example, your team may play a Thursday night game during a particular week), the workouts are not always performed on the same day.

DATES: July 28–September 7
CYCLE: In-Season I
GOAL: Maintain power during the competitive phase because of the positive relationship between muscle power and performance.
LENGTH: 6 weeks
INTENSITY: Select a resistance that allows for completion of the full number of required repetitions on the *first* set only prior to increasing resistance.
PACE: Perform total-body lifts explosively. For all other exercises, lift in 1.5 seconds and lower in 2 seconds.
REST: 2:00 between total-body exercises, 1:30 between all other sets and exercises
SETS/REPS:

- July 28–Aug 3: TB=3x2, CL=3x3, AL=3x5
- Aug 4–Aug 10: TB=3x4, CL=3x5, AL=3x5
- Aug 11–Aug 17: TB=3x2, CL=3x3, AL=3x5
- Aug 18–Aug 24: TB=3x4, CL=3x5, AL=3x5
- Aug 25–Aug 31: TB=3x2, CL=3x3, AL=3x5
- Sept 1–Sept 7: TB=3x4, CL=3x5, AL=3x5

Day 2
DATES: July 28–September 7
CYCLE: In-Season I
GOAL: Maintain power during the competitive phase because of the positive relationship between muscle power and performance.
LENGTH: 6 weeks
INTENSITY: Select a resistance that allows for completion of the full number of required repetitions on the *first* set only prior to increasing resistance.
PACE: Perform total-body lifts explosively. For all other exercises, lift in 1.5 seconds and lower in 2 seconds.
REST: 2:00 between total body exercises, 1:30 between all other sets and exercises
SETS/REPS:

- July 28–Aug 3: TB=3x4, TL=3x5@7 sec (1.4)
- Aug 4–Aug 10: TB=3x2, TL=3x3@3 sec (1)
- Aug 11–Aug 17: TB=3x4, TL=3x5@7 sec (1.4)
- Aug 18–Aug 24: TB=3x2, TL=3x3@3 sec (1)
- Aug 25–Aug 31: TB=3x4, TL=3x5@7 sec (1.4)
- Sept 1–Sept 7: TB=3x2, TL=3x3@3 sec (1)

	Week 1	Week 2	Week 3	Week 4	Week 5	Week 6
TOTAL BODY (CHOOSE 1) Bar/DB/Tire Hang Squat Cleans TB WT Lifted	3x2	3x4	3x2	3x4	3x2	3x4
Bar/DB Hang Split ALT FT Snatch TB WT Lifted	3x2	3x4	3x2	3x4	3x2	3x4
DB Hang Squat ALT Clean TB WT Lifted	3x2	3x4	3x2	3x4	3x2	3x4
LOWER BODY (CHOOSE 2+Stabilization) Bar/DB/Keg/Log Squats CL WT Lifted (Partial First Set)	3x3	3x5	3x3	3x5	3x3	3x5
DB Lateral Step-Up/Crossover Off CL WT Lifted (Total)	3x3	3x5	3x3	3x5	3x3	3x5
Leg Curls AL WT Lifted	3x3	3x5	3x3	3x5	3x3	3x5
60-Second Stabilization Each Leg	1x60 sec	1x60 sec	1x60 sec	1x60 sec	1x60 sec	1x60 sec
TRUNK (PERFORM BOTH) Sit Fit 1-Leg Ankle Chop WT Lifted	3x10	3x10	3x10	3x10	3x10	3x10
Keg Lift WT Lifted	3x8	3x8	3x8	3x8	3x8	3x8
CHEST/SHOULDERS (CHOOSE 2) Bar/DB/Keg/Log Bench Press WT Lifted (Partial First Set)	3x3	3x5	3x3	3x5	3x3	3x5
DB/Keg/Log Incline (Total) Wt Lifted (Partial First Set)	3x3	3x5	3x3	3x5	3x3	3x5
NECK MR Flexion/Extension Reps Completed	2x8	2x8	2x8	2x8	2x8	2x8
ROTATOR CUFF Functional Rotation Reps Completed	2x8	2x8	2x8	2x8	2x8	2x8

Day 1 Workout Regimen

	Week 1	Week 2	Week 3	Week 4	Week 5	Week 6
TOTAL BODY (CHOOSE 1) Bar/DB Split ALT FT Jerk TB WT Lifted	3x4 ____	3x2@65% ____	3x4@55% ____	3x2@65% ____	3x4@55% ____	3x4@65% ____
DB Split ALT FT ALT Jerk TB WT Lifted	3x4 ____	3x2@65% ____	3x4@55% ____	3x2@65% ____	3x4@55% ____	3x4@65% ____
Bar/DB Hang ALT FT ALT Snatch TB WT Lifted	3x4 ____	3x2@65% ____	3x4@55% ____	3x2@65% ____	3x4@55% ____	3x4@65% ____
LOWER BODY (CHOOSE 1) Bar/DB/Keg/Log Squat CL WT Lifted (Partial First Set)	3x5@7 sec ____	3x3@3 sec ____	3x5@7 sec ____	3x3@3 sec ____	3x5@7 sec ____	3x3@3 sec ____
Bar/DB/Keg/Log Side Lunges CL WT Lifted (Total)	3x5@7 sec ____	3x3@3 sec ____	3x5@7 sec ____	3x3@3 sec ____	3x5@7 sec ____	3x3@3 sec ____
Bar/DB/Keg/Log SLDL CL WT Lifted	3x5@7 sec ____	3x3@3 sec ____	3x5@7 sec ____	3x3@3 sec ____	3x5@7 sec ____	3x3@3 sec ____
TRUNK (PERFORM BOTH) MB 1-Leg Twist Throws WT Lifted	3x10 ____	3x10 ____	3x10 ____	3x10 ____	3x10 ____	3x10 ____
WT Twist 1-Leg Glute Ham WT Lifted	3x8 ____	3x8 ____	3x8 ____	3x8 ____	3x8 ____	3x8 ____
CHEST/SHOULDER (CHOOSE 1) Bar/DB/Keg/Log Bench Press WT Lifted (Partial First Set)	3x5@7 sec ____	3x3@3 sec ____	3x5@7 sec ____	3x3@3 sec ____	3x5@7 sec ____	3x3@3 sec ____
Bar/DB/Keg/Log Incline Press CL WT Lifted (Partial First Set)	3x5@7 sec ____	3x3@3 sec ____	3x5@7 sec ____	3x3@3 sec ____	3x5@7 sec ____	3x3@3 sec ____
Bar/DB/Keg/Log Incline Press CL WT Lifted (Partial First Set)	3x5@7 sec ____	3x3@3 sec ____	3x5@7 sec ____	3x3@3 sec ____	3x5@7 sec ____	3x3@3 sec ____
NECK MR Lateral Flexion Reps Completed	2x8 ____	2x8 ____	2x8 ____	2x8 ____	2x8 ____	2x8 ____
ROTATOR CUFF Empty Cans Reps Completed	2x8 ____	2x8 ____	2x8 ____	2x8 ____	2x8 ____	2x8 ____

Day 2 Workout Regimen

In-Season Cycle II

RUNNING BACK/WIDE RECEIVER

Day 1
DATES: Sept 8–Oct 19
CYCLE: In-Season II
GOAL: Increase strength and power during the competitive season.
LENGTH: 6 weeks
INTENSITY: Select a resistance that allows for completion of the full number of required repetitions on the *first* set only prior to increasing resistance.
PACE: Perform total-body lifts explosively. For all other exercises, lift in 1.5 seconds and lower in 2 seconds.
REST: 2:30 between total-body exercises, 2:00 between all other sets and exercises
SETS/REPS:

- Sept 8–Sept 14: TB=3x5, CL=3x4, AL=3x6
- Sept 15–Sept 21: TB=3x3, CL=3x2, AL=3x6
- Sept 22–Sept 28: TB=3x5, CL=3x4, AL=3x6
- Sept 29–Oct 5: TB=3x3, CL=3x2, AL=3x6
- Oct 6–Oct 12: TB=3x5, CL=3x4, AL=3x6
- Oct 13–Oct 19: TB=3x3, CL=3x2, AL=3x6

Day 2
DATES: Sept 8–Oct 19
CYCLE: In-Season II
GOAL: Increase strength and power during the competitive season.
LENGTH: 6 weeks
INTENSITY: Select a resistance that allows for completion of the full number of required repetitions on the *first* set only prior to increasing resistance.
PACE: Perform total-body lifts explosively. For all other exercises, lift in 1.5 seconds and lower in 2 seconds.
REST: 2:30 between total-body exercises, 2:00 between all other sets and exercises
SETS/REPS:

- Sept 8–Sept 14: TB=3x3, TL=3x2@2 sec (1)
- Sept 15–Sept 21: TB=3x5, TL=3x4@6 sec (1.5)
- Sept 22–Sept 28: TB=3x3, TL=3x2@2 sec (1)
- Sept 29–Oct 5: TB=3x5, TL=3x4@6 sec(1.5)
- Oct 6–Oct 12: TB=3x3, TL=3x2@2 sec (1)
- Oct 13–Oct 19: TB=3x5, TL=3x4@6 sec(1.5)

	Week 1	Week 2	Week 3	Week 4	Week 5	Week 6
TOTAL BODY (CHOOSE 1)						
Bar/DB Hang Split ALT FT Snatch TB WT Lifted	3x5 ____	3x3 ____	3x5 ____	3x3 ____	3x5 ____	3x3 ____
DB CMD Hang Split ALT FT Snatch TB WT Lifted	3x5 ____	3x3 ____	3x5 ____	3x3 ____	3x5 ____	3x3 ____
Bar/DB Split ALT FT Jerks TB WT Lifted	3x5 ____	3x3 ____	3x5 ____	3x3 ____	3x5 ____	3x3 ____
LOWER BODY (CHOOSE 2+Stabilization)						
Bar/DB/Keg/Log Squats CL WT Lifted (Partial First Set)	3x4 ____	3x2 ____	3x4 ____	3x2 ____	3x4 ____	3x2 ____
DB Lateral Step-Up/Lateral Step-Off CL WT Lifted (Total)	3x4 ____	3x2 ____	3x4 ____	3x2 ____	3x4 ____	3x2 ____
Bar/DB/Keg/Log RDL CL WT Lifted	3x4 ____	3x2 ____	3x4 ____	3x2 ____	3x4 ____	3x2 ____
60-Second Stabilization Each Leg	1x60 sec ____	1x60 sec ____	1x60 sec ____	1x60 sec ____	1x60 sec ____	1x60 sec ____
TRUNK (PERFORM BOTH)						
WT Bicycles WT Lifted	3x10 ____	3x10 ____	3x10 ____	3x10 ____	3x10 ____	3x10 ____
WT Twist 1-Leg Back Extensions WT Lifted	3x8 ____	3x8 ____	3x8 ____	3x8 ____	3x8 ____	3x8 ____
CHEST/SHOULDERS (CHOOSE 2)						
DB/Keg/Log Incline CL (Partial First Set) WT Lifted	3x4 ____	3x2 ____	3x4 ____	3x2 ____	3x4 ____	3x2 ____
Bar/DB/Keg/Log Shoulder Press CL WT Lifted (Partial First Set)	3x4 ____	3x2 ____	3x4 ____	3x2 ____	3x4 ____	3x2 ____
Standing Bar Press CL WT Lifted (Partials) (Each Arm)	3x4 ____	3x2 ____	3x4 ____	3x2 ____	3x4 ____	3x2 ____
NECK MR Flexion/Extension Reps Completed	2x8 ____	2x8 ____	2x8 ____	2x8 ____	2x8 ____	2x8 ____

Day 1 Workout Regimen

	Week 1	Week 2	Week 3	Week 4	Week 5	Week 6
TOTAL BODY (CHOOSE 1) Bar/DB Split ALT FT Jerks TB WT Lifted	3x3 ___	3x5@55% ___	3x3@65% ___	3x5@55% ___	3x3@65% ___	3x5@55% ___
Bar/Tire Hang Squat Cleans TB WT Lifted	3x3@65% ___	3x5@55% ___	3x3@65% ___	3x5@55% ___	3x3@65% ___	3x5@55% ___
DB Hang Squat ALT Clean TB WT Lifted	3x3 ___	3x5@55% ___	3x3@65% ___	3x5@55% ___	3x3@65% ___	3x5@55% ___
LOWER BODY (CHOOSE 1) Bar/DB/Keg/Log Squats TL WT Lifted	3x2@2 sec ___	3x4@6 sec ___	3x2@2 sec ___	3x4@6 sec ___	3x2@2 sec ___	3x4@6 sec ___
Bar/DB/Keg/Log Side Lunge TL WT Lifted (Total)	3x2@2 sec ___	3x4@6 sec ___	3x2@2 sec ___	3x4@6 sec ___	3x2@2 sec ___	3x4@6 sec ___
Leg Curl TL WT Lifted	3x2@2 sec ___	3x4@6 sec ___	3x2@2 sec ___	3x4@6 sec ___	3x2@2 sec ___	3x4@6 sec ___
TRUNK (PERFORM BOTH) Sit Fit 1-Leg Chop Throws WT Lifted	3x10 ___	3x10 ___	3x10 ___	3x10 ___	3x10 ___	3x10 ___
WT 1-Leg Back Extensions WT Lifted	3x8 ___	3x8 ___	3x8 ___	3x8 ___	3x8 ___	3x8 ___
CHEST/SHOULDERS (CHOOSE 1) Bar/DB/Keg/Log Bench TL (Partial First Set) WT Lifted	3x2@2 sec ___	3x4@6 sec ___	3x2@2 sec ___	3x4@6 sec ___	3x2@2 sec ___	3x4@6 sec ___
Bar/DB Upright Row TL WT Lifted	3x2@2 sec ___	3x4@6 sec ___	3x2@2 sec ___	3x4@6 sec ___	3x2@2 sec ___	3x4@6 sec ___
NECK MR Lateral Flexion Reps Completed	2x8 ___	2x8 ___	2x8 ___	2x8 ___	2x8 ___	2x8 ___

Day 2 Workout Regimen

In-Season Cycle III

DEFENSIVE BACKS

Day 1
DATES: Oct 20–Nov 22
CYCLE: In-Season III
GOAL: Increase strength and power during the competitive season.
LENGTH: 5 weeks
INTENSITY: Select a resistance that allows for completion of the full number of required repetitions on the *first* set only prior to increasing resistance.
PACE: Perform total-body lifts explosively. For all other exercises, lift in 1.5 seconds and lower in 2 seconds.
REST: 2:30 between total-body exercises, 2:00 between all other sets and exercises
SETS/REPS:
- Oct 20–Oct 26: TB=3x2, CL=3x3, AL=3x5
- Oct 27–Nov 2: TB=3x4, CL=3x5, AL=3x5
- Nov 3–Nov 9: TB=3x2, CL=3x3, AL=3x5
- Nov 10–Nov 16: TB=3x4, CL=3x5, AL=3x5
- Nov 17–Nov 22: TB=3x2, CL=3x3, AL=3x5

	Week 1	Week 2	Week 3	Week 4	Week 5
TOTAL BODY (CHOOSE 1) Bar/DB Split ALT FT Jerks TB WT Lifted	3x2 ____	3x4 ____	3x2 ____	3x4 ____	3x4 ____
Bar/DB Hang Split ALT FT ALT Snatch TB WT Lifted	3x2 ____	3x4 ____	3x2 ____	3x4 ____	3x4 ____
LOWER BODY (PERFORM ALL) Bar/DB/Keg/Log Squats CL WT Lifted	3x3 ____	3x5 ____	3x3 ____	3x5 ____	3x5 ____
Bar/DB/Keg/Log SLDL CL WT Lifted (Total)	3x3 ____	3x5 ____	3x3 ____	3x5 ____	3x5 ____
1x60-Second Stabilization Each Leg	1x60 sec ____	1x60 sec ____	1x60 sec ____	1x60 sec ____	1x60 sec ____
TRUNK (PERFORM BOTH) MB Decline Push-Downs WT Lifted	3x10 ____	3x10 ____	3x10 ____	3x10 ____	3x10 ____
WT Twist 1-Leg Glute Ham WT Lifted	3x8 ____	3x8 ____	3x8 ____	3x8 ____	3x8 ____
CHEST/SHOULDERS (PERFORM BOTH) Bar/DB/Log/Keg/Bench CL (Partial First Set) WT Lifted	3x3 ____	3x5 ____	3x3 ____	3x5 ____	3x5 ____
Bar/DB Upright Row CL WT Lifted	3x3 ____	3x5 ____	3x3 ____	3x5 ____	3x5 ____
NECK MR Flexion/Extension Reps Completed	2x8 ____	2x8 ____	2x8 ____	2x8 ____	2x8 ____

Day 1 Workout Regimen

Day 2

DATES: Oct 20–Nov 22
CYCLE: In-Season III
GOAL: Increase strength and power during the competitive season.
LENGTH: 5 weeks
INTENSITY: Select a resistance that allows for completion of the full number of required repetitions on the first set only prior to increasing resistance.
PACE: Perform total-body lifts explosively. For all other exercises, lift in 1.5 seconds and lower in 2 seconds.
REST: 2:30 between total-body exercises, 2:00 between all other sets and exercises
SETS/REPS:
- Oct 20–Oct 26: TB=3x4, TL=3x5@7 sec (1.4)
- Oct 27–Nov 2: TB=3x2, TL=3x3@3 sec (1)
- Nov 3–Nov 9: TB=3x4, TL=3x5@7 sec (1.4)
- Nov 10–Nov 16: TB=3x2, TL=3x3@3 sec (1)
- Nov 17–Nov 22: TB=3x4, TL=3x5@7 sec (1.4)

	Week 1	Week 2	Week 3	Week 4	Week 5
TOTAL BODY (CHOOSE 1) Bar/DB/Tire Hang Squat Cleans TB WT Lifted	3x4 ___	3x2@65% ___	3x4@75% ___	3x2@65% ___	3x4@75% ___
DB Hang Squat ALT Cleans TB WT Lifted	3x4 ___	3x2@65% ___	3x4@75% ___	3x2@65% ___	3x4@75% ___
LOWER BODY (CHOOSE 1) DB/Keg/Log Reverse Lunges TL WT Lifted (Total)	3x5@7 sec ___	3x3@3 sec ___	3x5@7 sec ___	3x3@3 sec ___	3x5@7 sec ___
DB/Keg/Log SLDL TL WT Lifted	3x5@7 sec ___	3x3@3 sec ___	3x5@7 sec ___	3x3@3 sec ___	3x5@7 sec ___
TRUNK (PERFORM BOTH) Sit Fit 1-Leg Wood Chops WT Lifted	3x10 ___	3x10 ___	3x10 ___	3x10 ___	3x10 ___
Keg Lift WT Lifted	3x8 ___	3x8 ___	3x8 ___	3x8 ___	3x8 ___
CHEST/SHOULDERS (CHOOSE 1) Standing Bar Press TL WT Lifted (Partial First Set)	3x5@7 sec ___	3x3@3 sec ___	3x5@7 sec ___	3x3@3 sec ___	3x5@7 sec ___
DB/Keg/Log Shoulder Press TL WT Lifted	3x5@7 sec ___	3x3@3 sec ___	3x5@7 sec ___	3x3@3 sec ___	3x5@7 sec ___
NECK MR Lateral Flexion Reps Completed	2x8 ___	2x8 ___	2x8 ___	2x8 ___	2x8 ___

Day 2 Workout Regimen

Training Cycles

NON-SKILL-POSITION ATHLETES

DATES: Nov 25–Jan 5
CYCLE: Pre-Introduction (freshmen only)
GOAL: Introduce athletes to the demands of resistance training and emphasize correct technique.
LENGTH: 6 weeks
INTENSITY: Select a resistance that allows for completion of the full number of required repetitions on *each* set prior to increasing resistance.
PACE: Perform total-body lifts explosively. For all other exercises, lift in 2 seconds and lower in 4 seconds.
REST: 2:00 between sets and exercises
SETS/REPS:
Nov 25–Dec 1: TB=3x7, CL=3x11, AL=3x11
- Dec 2–Dec 8: TB=3x4, CL=3x8, AL=3x8
- Dec 9–Dec 15: TB=3x7, CL=3x11, AL=3x11
- Dec 16–Dec 22: TB=3x4, CL=3x8, AL=3x8
- Dec 23–Dec 29: TB=3x7, CL=3x11, AL=3x11
- Dec 30–Jan 5: TB=3x4, CL=3x8, AL=3x8

DATES: Jan 6–Jan 12
CYCLE: Introduction
GOAL: Reintroduce athletes to the demands of resistance training and emphasize correct technique.
LENGTH: 1 week
INTENSITY: Select a resistance that allows for completion of the full number of required repetitions on *each* set prior to increasing resistance.
PACE: Perform total-body lifts explosively. For all other exercises, lift in 2 seconds and lower in 4 seconds.
REST: 2:00 between sets and exercises
SETS/REPS:
- Jan 6–Jan 12: TB=3x7, CL=3x11, AL=3x11

DATES: Jan 13–Feb 9
CYCLE: Strength I
GOAL: Increase muscle strength, because of the positive relationship between muscle strength and power.
LENGTH: 4 weeks
INTENSITY: Select a resistance that allows for completion of the full number of required repetitions on *each* set prior to increasing resistance.
PACE: Perform total-body lifts explosively. For all other exercises, lift in 2 seconds and lower in 3 seconds.
REST: 2:00 between all sets and exercises
SETS/REPS:
- Jan 13–Jan 19: TB=3x6, CL=3x9, AL=3x9
- Jan 20–Jan 26: TB=4x3, CL=4x7, AL=3x7

- Jan 27–Feb 2: TB=4x6, CL=4x9, AL=3x9
- Feb 3–Feb 9: TB=4x3, CL=4x7, AL=3x7

DATES: Feb 10–March 23
CYCLE: Strength II
GOAL: Increase muscle strength, because of the positive relationship between strength and power.
LENGTH: 6 weeks
INTENSITY: Select a resistance that allows for completion of the full number of required repetitions on the *first* set only prior to increasing resistance.
PACE: Perform total-body lifts explosively. For all other exercises, lift in 2 seconds and lower in 3 seconds.
REST: 2:30 between total-body exercises, 2:00 between all other sets and exercises
SETS/REPS:
- Feb 10–Feb 16: TB=4x5, CL=4x6, AL=3x6
- Feb 17–Feb 23: TB=4x3, CL=4x4, AL=3x6
- Feb 24–March 2: TB=4x5, CL=4x6, AL=3x6
- March 3–March 9: TB=4x3, CL=4x4, AL=3x6
- March 10–March 16: TB=4x5, CL=4x6, AL=3x6
- March 17–March 23: TB=4x3, CL=4x4, AL=3x6

DATES: March 31–April 27
CYCLE: Spring Practice
GOAL: Increase strength and power during the competitive season.
LENGTH: 4 weeks
INTENSITY: For total-body exercises, select a resistance that allows for completion of the full number of required repetitions on the *first* set only prior to increasing resistance. For timed exercises, reduce the resistance as necessary to maintain the desired speed of movement during each set.
PACE: Perform total-body lifts explosively. Perform timed lifts at a pace that allows for completion of the required number of repetitions in the specified time period.
REST: 3:00 between total-body exercises, 2:30 between all other sets and exercises
SETS/REPS:
- March 31–April 6: TB=3x2, TL=3x3@8 sec (2.7)
- April 7–April 13: TB=3x4, TL=3x6@12 sec (2)
- April 14–April 20: TB=3x2, TL=3x3@8 sec (2.7)
- April 21–April 27: TB=3x4, TL=3x6@12 sec (2)

DATES: April 28–May 18
CYCLE: Strength III
GOAL: Increase muscle strength, because of the positive relationship between strength and power.
LENGTH: 3 weeks
INTENSITY: Select a resistance that allows for completion of the full number of required repetitions on the *first* set only prior to increasing resistance.
PACE: Perform total-body lifts explosively. For all other exercises, lift in 2 seconds and lower in 3 seconds.

REST: 2:30 between total-body exercises, 2:00 between all other sets and exercises
SETS/REPS:
- April 28–May 4: TB=4x3, CL=4x3, AL=3x8
- May 5–May 11: TB=4x5, CL=4x5, AL=3x8
- May 12–May 18: TB=4x3, CL=4x3, AL=3x8

DATES: May 19–June 8
CYCLE: Strength IV
GOAL: Further increase strength, because of the relationship between strength and power.
LENGTH: 3 weeks
INTENSITY: Select a resistance that allows for completion of the full number of required repetitions on the *first* set only prior to increasing resistance.
PACE: Perform total-body lifts explosively. For all other exercises, lift in 1.5 seconds and lower in 2 seconds.
REST: 2:30 between total-body exercises, 2:00 between all other sets and exercises
SETS/REPS:
- May 19–May 25: TB=4x4, CL=4x4, AL=3x6
- May 26–June 1: TB=4x2, CL=4x2, AL=3x6
- June 2–June 8: TB=4x4, CL=4x4, AL=3x6

DATES: June 9–July 6
CYCLE: Power I
GOAL: Increase muscle power, because of the positive relationship between muscle power and performance.
LENGTH: 4 weeks
INTENSITY: For total-body exercises, select a resistance that allows for completion of the full number of required repetitions on the *first* set only prior to increasing resistance. For timed exercises, reduce the resistance as necessary to maintain the desired speed of movement during each set.
PACE: Perform total-body lifts explosively. Perform timed lifts at a pace that allows for completion of the required number of repetitions in the specified time period.
REST: 3:00 between total-body exercises, 2:30 between all other sets and exercises
SETS/REPS:
- June 9–June 15: TB=5x3, TL=4x6@13 sec (2.2)
- June 16–June 22: TB=5x2, TL=4x3@6 sec (2)
- June 23–June 29: TB=5x3, TL=4x6@13 sec (2.2)
- June 30–July 6: TB=5x2, TL=4x3@6 sec (2)

DATES: July 7–July 27
CYCLE: Power II
GOAL: Further increase muscle power, because of the positive relationship between muscle power and performance.
LENGTH: 3 weeks
INTENSITY: For total-body exercises, select a resistance that allows for completion of the full number of required repetitions on the *first* set only prior to increasing resistance. For timed exercises, reduce the resistance as necessary to maintain the desired speed of movement during each set.

PACE: Perform total-body lifts explosively. Perform timed lifts at a pace that allows for completion of the required number of repetitions in the specified time period. For all other exercises, lift in 2 seconds and lower in 3 seconds.
REST: 3:00 between total-body exercises, 2:30 between all other sets and exercises
SETS/REPS:
- July 7–July 13: TB=5x3, TL=4x4@7 sec (1.6)
- July 14–July 20: TB=5x2, TL=4x2@3 sec (1.4)
- July 21–July 27: TB=5x1, TL=4x2@3 sec (1.4)

DATES: July 28–Sept 7
CYCLE: In-Season I
GOAL: Increase strength and power during the competitive season.
LENGTH: 6 weeks
INTENSITY: Complete the full number of repetitions in good form on the *first* set only prior to increasing resistance.
PACE: Perform total-body lifts as explosively as possible. For all other exercises, lift in 1.5 seconds and lower in 2 seconds.
REST: 2:00 minutes between total-body exercises, 1:30 between all other exercises
SETS/REPS:
- July 28–Aug 3: TB=3x2, CL=3x3, AL=3x5
- Aug 4–Aug 10: TB=3x4, CL=3x5, AL=3x5
- Aug 11–Aug 17: TB=3x2, CL=3x3, AL=3x5
- Aug 18–Aug 24: TB=3x4, CL=3x5, AL=3x5
- Aug 25–Aug 31: TB=3x2, CL=3x3, AL=3x5
- Sept 1–Sept 7: TB=3x4, CL=3x5, AL=3x5

DATES: Sept 8–Oct 19
CYCLE: In-Season II
GOAL: Increase strength and power during the competitive season.
LENGTH: 6 weeks
INTENSITY: Complete the full number of repetitions in good form on the *first* set only prior to increasing resistance.
PACE: Perform total-body lifts as explosively as possible. For all other exercises, lift in 1.5 seconds and lower in 2 seconds
REST: 2:00 minutes between total-body exercises, 1:30 between all other exercises
SETS/REPS:
- Sept 8–Sept 14: TB=3x3, CL=3x2, AL=3x5
- Sept 15–Sept 21: TB=3x5, CL=3x4, AL=3x5
- Sept 22–Sept 28: TB=3x3, CL=3x2, AL=3x5
- Sept 29–Oct 5: TB=3x5, CL=3x4, AL=3x5
- Oct 6–Oct 12: TB=3x3, CL=3x2, AL=3x5
- Oct 13–Oct 19: TB=3x5, CL=3x4, AL=3x5

DATES: Oct 20–Nov 22
CYCLE: In-Season III
GOAL: Increase strength and power during the competitive season.
LENGTH: 5 weeks

INTENSITY: Complete the full number of repetitions in good form on the *first* set only prior to increasing resistance.

PACE: Perform total-body lifts as explosively as possible. For all other exercises, lift in 1.5 seconds and lower in 2 seconds.

REST: 2:00 minutes between total-body exercises, 1:30 between all other exercises

SETS/REPS:
- Oct 20–Oct 26: TB=3x2, CL=3x3, AL=3x5
- Oct 27–Nov 2: TB=3x4, CL=3x5, AL=3x3
- Nov 3–Nov 9: TB=3x2, CL=3x3, AL=3x5
- Nov 10–Nov 16: TB=3x4, CL=3x5, AL=3x3
- Nov 17–Nov 22: TB=3x2, CL=3x3, AL=3x5

Well-designed strength and conditioning programs, coupled with hardworking athletes, are a prerequisite for success.

Pre-Introduction Cycle

OFFENSIVE LINEMEN/TIGHT ENDS

Monday/Thursday
DATES: Nov 25–Jan 5
CYCLE: Pre-Introduction (freshmen only)
GOAL: Introduce athletes to the demands of resistance training and emphasize correct technique.
LENGTH: 6 weeks
INTENSITY: Select a resistance that allows for completion of the full number of required repetitions on *each* set prior to increasing resistance.
PACE: Perform total-body lifts explosively. For all other exercises, lift in 2 seconds and lower in 4 seconds.
REST: 2:00 between sets and exercises
SETS/REPS:

- Nov 25–Dec 1: TB=3x7, CL=3x11, AL=3x11
- Dec 2–Dec 8: TB=3x4, CL=3x8, AL=3x8
- Dec 9–Dec 15: TB=3x7, CL=3x11, AL=3x11
- Dec 16–Dec 22: TB=3x4, CL=3x8, AL=3x8
- Dec 23–Dec 29: TB=3x7, CL=3x11, AL=3x11
- Dec 30–Jan 5: TB=3x4, CL=3x8, AL=3x8

	Week 1 MON	Week 2 THURS	Week 3 MON	Week 4 THURS	Week 5 MON	Week 6 THURS
TOTAL BODY DB Squat Clean (Shin) TB WT Lifted	3x7 ___	3x4 ___	3x7 ___	3x4 ___	3x7 ___	3x4 ___
CHEST DB Bench Press CL WT Lifted	3x11 ___	3x8 ___	3x11 ___	3x8 ___	3x11 ___	3x8 ___
DB Pull-Over CL WT Lifted	3x11 ___	3x8 ___	3x11 ___	3x8 ___	3x11 ___	3x8 ___
TRUNK WT Crunch WT Lifted	3x20 ___	3x20 ___	3x20 ___	3x20 ___	3x20 ___	3x20 ___
WT Twist Crunch WT Lifted	3x20 ___	3x20 ___	3x20 ___	3x20 ___	3x20 ___	3x20 ___
WT Back Extensions WT Lifted	3x15 ___	3x15 ___	3x15 ___	3x15 ___	3x15 ___	3x15 ___
SHOULDERS DB Upright Row CL WT Lifted	3x11 ___	3x8 ___	3x11 ___	3x8 ___	3x11 ___	3x8 ___
DB Lateral Raise AL WT Lifted	3x11 ___	3x8 ___	3x11 ___	3x8 ___	3x11 ___	3x8 ___

Monday/Thursday Workout Regimen

Tuesday/Friday

DATES: Nov 25–Jan 5
CYCLE: Pre-Introduction (freshmen only)
GOAL: Introduce athletes to the demands of resistance training and emphasize correct technique.
LENGTH: 6 weeks
INTENSITY: Select a resistance that allows for completion of the full number of required repetitions on *each* set prior to increasing resistance.
PACE: Perform total-body lifts explosively. For all other exercises, lift in 2 seconds and lower in 4 seconds.
REST: 2:00 between sets and exercises
SETS/REPS:

- Nov 25–Dec 1: TB=3x7, CL=3x11, AL=3x11
- Dec 2–Dec 8: TB=3x4, CL=3x8, AL=3x8
- Dec 9–Dec 15: TB=3x7, CL=3x11, AL=3x11
- Dec 16–Dec 22: TB=3x4, CL=3x8, AL=3x8
- Dec 23–Dec 29: TB=3x7, CL=3x11, AL=3x11
- Dec 30–Jan 5: TB=3x4, CL=3x8, AL=3x8

	Week 1 TUES	Week 2 FRI	Week 3 TUES	Week 4 FRI	Week 5 TUES	Week 6 FRI
TOTAL BODY Push Press TB WT Lifted	3x7 ___	3x4 ___	3x7 ___	3x4 ___	3x7 ___	3x4 ___
LOWER BODY Squats CL WT Lifted	3x11 ___	3x8 ___	3x11 ___	3x8 ___	3x11 ___	3x8 ___
Leg Curl/MR Leg Curl AL WT Lifted	3x11/2x8 ___	3x8/2x8 ___	3x11/2x8 ___	3x8/2x8 ___	3x11/2x8 ___	3x8/2x8 ___
TRUNK WT Toe Touch WT Lifted	3x20 ___	3x20 ___	3x20 ___	3x20 ___	3x20 ___	3x20 ___
Trunk Twist Reps Completed	3x20 ___	3x20 ___	3x20 ___	3x20 ___	3x20 ___	3x20 ___
UPPER BACK Seated Row/PD/T-Bar CL WT Lifted	3x11 ___	3x8 ___	3x11 ___	3x8 ___	3x11 ___	3x8 ___
BICEPS Any Biceps AL WT Lifted	3x11 ___	3x8 ___	3x11 ___	3x8 ___	3x11 ___	3x8 ___
NECK MR Flexion/Extension Reps Completed	2x8 ___	2x8 ___	2x8 ___	2x8 ___	2x8 ___	2x8 ___

Tuesday/Friday Workout Regimen

Thursday/Monday

DATES: Nov 25–Jan 5
CYCLE: Pre-Introduction (freshmen only)
GOAL: Introduce athletes to the demands of resistance training and emphasize correct technique.
LENGTH: 6 weeks
INTENSITY: Select a resistance that allows for completion of the full number of required repetitions on *each* set prior to increasing resistance.
PACE: Perform total-body lifts explosively. For all other exercises, lift in 2 seconds and lower in 4 seconds.
REST: 2:00 between sets and exercises
SETS/REPS:

- Nov 25–Dec 1: TB=3x4, CL=3x8, AL=3x8
- Dec 2–Dec 8: TB=3x7, CL=3x11, AL=3x11
- Dec 9–Dec 15: TB=3x4, CL=3x8, AL=3x8
- Dec 16–Dec 22: TB=3x7, CL=3x11, AL=3x11
- Dec 23–Dec 29: TB=3x4, CL=3x8, AL=3x8
- Dec 30–Jan 5: TB=3x7, CL=3x11, AL=3x11

	Week 1 THURS	Week 2 MON	Week 3 THURS	Week 4 MON	Week 5 THURS	Week 6 MON
TOTAL BODY Squat Clean (FLR) TB WT Lifted	3x4 ___	3x7 ___	3x4 ___	3x7 ___	3x4 ___	3x7 ___
UPPER BODY Bench Press CL WT Lifted	3x8 ___	3x11 ___	3x8 ___	3x11 ___	3x8 ___	3x11 ___
Incline Press CL WT Lifted	3x8 ___	3x11 ___	3x8 ___	3x11 ___	3x8 ___	3x11 ___
TRUNK WT V-Up WT Lifted	3x20 ___	3x20 ___	3x20 ___	3x20 ___	3x20 ___	3x20 ___
WT Seated Twist WT Lifted	3x20 ___	3x20 ___	3x20 ___	3x20 ___	3x20 ___	3x20 ___
WT Twist Back Extension WT Lifted	3x15 ___	3x15 ___	3x15 ___	3x15 ___	3x15 ___	3x15 ___
SHOULDERS Upright Row CL WT Lifted	3x8 ___	3x11 ___	3x8 ___	3x11 ___	3x8 ___	3x11 ___
Squat Plate Raise AL WT Lifted	3x8 ___	3x11 ___	3x8 ___	3x11 ___	3x8 ___	3x11 ___

Thursday/Monday Workout Regimen

Friday/Tuesday

DATES: Nov 25–Jan 5
CYCLE: Pre-Introduction (freshmen only)
GOAL: Introduce athletes to the demands of resistance training and emphasize correct technique.
LENGTH: 6 weeks
INTENSITY: Select a resistance that allows for completion of the full number of required repetitions on *each* set prior to increasing resistance.
PACE: Perform total-body lifts explosively. For all other exercises, lift in 2 seconds and lower in 4 seconds.
REST: 2:00 between sets and exercises
SETS/REPS:

- Nov 25–Dec 1: TB=3x4, CL=3x8, AL=3x8
- Dec 2–Dec 8: TB=3x7, CL=3x11, AL=3x11
- Dec 9–Dec 15: TB=3x4, CL=3x8, AL=3x8
- Dec 16–Dec 22: TB=3x7, CL=3x11, AL=3x11
- Dec 23–Dec 29: TB=3x4, CL=3x8, AL=3x8
- Dec 30–Jan 5: TB=3x7, CL=3x11, AL=3x11

	Week 1 FRI	Week 2 TUES	Week 3 FRI	Week 4 TUES	Week 5 FRI	Week 6 TUES
TOTAL BODY DB Push Press TB WT Lifted	3x4 ___	3x7 ___	3x4 ___	3x7 ___	3x4 ___	3x7 ___
LOWER BODY DB Squats CL WT Lifted	3x8 ___	3x11 ___	3x8 ___	3x11 ___	3x8 ___	3x11 ___
DB Lunge CL WT Lifted	3x8 ___	3x11 ___	3x8 ___	3x11 ___	3x8 ___	3x11 ___
TRUNK WT ALT V-Up WT Lifted	3x20 ___	3x20 ___	3x20 ___	3x20 ___	3x20 ___	3x20 ___
WT ALT Toe Touch WT Lifted	3x20 ___	3x20 ___	3x20 ___	3x20 ___	3x20 ___	3x20 ___
UPPER BACK DB Row CL WT Lifted	3x8 ___	3x11 ___	3x8 ___	3x11 ___	3x8 ___	3x11 ___
BICEPS Any DB Bicep AL WT Lifted	3x8 ___	3x11 ___	3x8 ___	3x11 ___	3x8 ___	3x11 ___
NECK MR Lateral Flexion Reps Completed	2x8 ___	2x8 ___	2x8 ___	2x8 ___	2x8 ___	2x8 ___

Friday/Tuesday Workout Regimen

Introduction Cycle

DEFENSIVE LINEMEN/LINEBACKERS

Monday
DATES: Jan 6–Jan 12
CYCLE: Introduction
GOAL: Reintroduce athletes to the demands of resistance training and emphasize correct technique.
LENGTH: 1 week
INTENSITY: Select a resistance that allows for completion of the full number of required repetitions on *each* set prior to increasing resistance.
PACE: Perform total-body lifts explosively. For all other exercises, lift in 2 seconds and lower in 4 seconds.
REST: 2:00 between sets and exercises
SETS/REPS:
- Jan 6–Jan 12: TB=3x5, CL=3x11, AL=3x11

	Week 1
TOTAL BODY Push Press TB WT Lifted	3x5 ____
LOWER BODY Squats CL WT Lifted	3x11 ____
Leg Curl/MR Leg Curl AL WT Lifted	3x11 ____
TRUNK WT Crunch WT Lifted	3x20 ____
WT Twist Crunch WT Lifted	3x20 ____
WT Back Extensions WT Lifted	3x15 ____
UPPER BACK Seated Row/PD/T-Bar CL WT Lifted	3x11 ____
BICEPS Any Biceps AL WT Lifted	3x11 ____

Monday Workout Regimen

Tuesday

DATES: Jan 6–Jan 12

CYCLE: Introduction

GOAL: Reintroduce athletes to the demands of resistance training and emphasize correct technique.

LENGTH: 1 week

INTENSITY: Select a resistance that allows for completion of the full number of required repetitions on each set prior to increasing resistance.

PACE: Perform total-body lifts explosively. For all other exercises, lift in 2 seconds and lower in 4 seconds.

REST: 2:00 between sets and exercises

SETS/REPS:
- Jan 6–Jan 12: TB=3x5, CL=3x11, AL=3x11

	Week 1
TOTAL BODY DB Push Press TB WT Lifted	3x5 _____
CHEST DB Bench Press CL WT Lifted	3x11 _____
DB Pull-Over CL WT Lifted	3x11 _____
TRUNK WT Toe Touch WT Lifted	3x20 _____
Trunk Twist Reps Completed	3x20 _____
SHOULDERS DB Front Raise CL WT Lifted	3x11 _____
DB Lateral Raise AL WT Lifted	3x11 _____
NECK MR Flexion/Extension Reps Completed	2x8 _____

Tuesday Workout Regimen

Thursday

DATES: Jan 6–Jan 12
CYCLE: Introduction
GOAL: Reintroduce athletes to the demands of resistance training and emphasize correct technique.
LENGTH: 1 week
INTENSITY: Select a resistance that allows for completion of the full number of required repetitions on each set prior to increasing resistance.
PACE: Perform total-body lifts explosively. For all other exercises, lift in 2 seconds and lower in 4 seconds.
REST: 2:00 between sets and exercises
SETS/REPS:
- Jan 6–Jan 12: TB=3x5, CL=3x11, AL=3x11

	Week 1
TOTAL BODY DB Squat Clean (Shin) TB WT Lifted	3x5 ____
LOWER BODY DB Squats CL WT Lifted	3x11 ____
DB Lunge CL (Total) WT Lifted	3x11 ____
TRUNK WT V-Up WT Lifted	3x20 ____
WT Bicycles WT Lifted	3x20 ____
WT Twist Back Extensions WT Lifted	3x15 ____
UPPER BACK DB Row CL WT Lifted	3x11 ____
BICEPS Any DB Biceps AL WT Lifted	3x11 ____

Thursday Workout Regimen

Friday

DATES: Jan 6–Jan 12

CYCLE: Introduction

GOAL: Reintroduce athletes to the demands of resistance training and emphasize correct technique.

LENGTH: 1 week

INTENSITY: Select a resistance that allows for completion of the full number of required repetitions on *each* set prior to increasing resistance.

PACE: Perform total-body lifts explosively. For all other exercises, lift in 2 seconds and lower in 4 seconds.

REST: 2:00 between sets and exercises

SETS/REPS:
- Jan 6–Jan 12: TB=3x5, CL=3x11, AL=3x11

	Week 1
TOTAL BODY Squat Cleans (FLR) TB WT Lifted	3x5 ____
UPPER BODY Bench Press CL WT Lifted Incline Press CL WT Lifted	3x11 ____ 3x11 ____
TRUNK MB Circles Reps Completed WT ALT Toe Touch WT Lifted	3x20 ____ 3x20 ____
SHOULDERS Upright Row CL WT Lifted Squat Plate Raise AL WT Lifted	3x11 ____ 3x11 ____
NECK MR Lateral Flexion Reps Completed	2x8 ____

Friday Workout Regimen

Strength Cycle I

FULLBACKS

Monday/Thursday
DATES: Jan 13–Feb 9
CYCLE: Strength I
GOAL: Increase muscle strength, because of the positive relationship between strength and power.
LENGTH: 4 weeks
INTENSITY: Select a resistance that allows for completion of the full number of required repetitions on *each* set prior to increasing resistance.
PACE: Perform total-body lifts explosively. For all other exercises, lift in 2 seconds and lower in 3 seconds.
REST: 2:00 between all sets and exercises
SETS/REPS:

- Jan 13–Jan 19: TB=3x6, CL=3x9, AL=3x9
- Jan 20–Jan 26: TB=4x3, CL=4x7, AL=3x7
- Jan 27–Feb 2: TB=4x6, CL=4x9, AL=3x9
- Feb 3–Feb 9: TB=4x3, CL=4x7, AL=3x7

	Week 1 MON	Week 2 THURS	Week 3 MON	Week 4 THURS
TOTAL BODY DB/Tire Squat Clean (Shin) TB WT Lifted	3x6 ___	4x3 ___	4x6 ___	4x3 ___
CHEST DB/Keg/Log Bench Press CL WT Lifted (Perform 1 Set Keg/Log)	3x9 ___	4x7 ___	4x9 ___	4x7 ___
DB/Keg/Log Incline CL WT Lifted (Perform 1 Set Keg/Log)	3x9 ___	4x7 ___	4x9 ___	4x7 ___
TRUNK WT Russian Twist WT Lifted	3x20 ___	3x20 ___	3x20 ___	3x20 ___
MB Overhead Crunch Reps Completed	3x20 ___	3x20 ___	3x20 ___	3x20 ___
WT Twist Glute Ham WT Lifted	3x10 ___	3x10 ___	3x10 ___	3x10 ___
SHOULDERS Squat Plate Raise CL WT Lifted	3x9 ___	4x7 ___	4x9 ___	4x7 ___
NECK MR Lateral Flexion Reps Completed	2x8 ___	2x8 ___	2x8 ___	2x8 ___

Monday/Thursday Workout Regimen

Tuesday/Friday

DATES: Jan 13–Feb 9
CYCLE: Strength I
GOAL: Increase muscle strength, because of the positive relationship between strength and power.
LENGTH: 4 weeks
INTENSITY: Select a resistance that allows for completion of the full number of required repetitions on *each* set prior to increasing resistance.
PACE: Perform total-body lifts explosively. For all other exercises, lift in 2 seconds and lower in 3 seconds.
REST: 2:00 between all sets and exercises
SETS/REPS:

- Jan 13–Jan 19: TB=3x6, CL=3x9, AL=3x9
- Jan 20–Jan 26: TB=4x3, CL=4x7, AL=3x7
- Jan 27–Feb 2: TB=4x6, CL=4x9, AL=3x9
- Feb 3–Feb 9: TB=4x3, CL=4x7, AL=3x7

	Week 1 TUES	Week 2 FRI	Week 3 TUES	Week 4 FRI
TOTAL BODY Split ALT Foot Snatch (FLR) TB WT Lifted	3x6 ___	4x3 ___	4x6 ___	4x3 ___
LOWER BODY Squats CL WT Lifted	3x9 ___	4x7 ___	4x9 ___	4x7 ___
Bar/Keg/Log RDL CL WT Lifted (Perform 1 Set Keg/Log)	3x9 ___	3x7 ___	3x9 ___	3x7 ___
TRUNK WT Toe Touch WT Lifted	3x20 ___	3x20 ___	3x20 ___	3x20 ___
WT Bicycles WT Lifted	3x20 ___	3x20 ___	3x20 ___	3x20 ___
UPPER BACK Seated Row/PD/T-Bar CL WT Lifted	3x9 ___	4x7 ___	4x9 ___	4x7 ___
BICEPS Any Bicep Exercise AL WT Lifted	3x9 ___	4x7 ___	4x9 ___	4x7 ___

Tuesday/Friday Workout Regimen

Thursday/Monday

DATES: Jan 13–Feb 9
CYCLE: Strength I
GOAL: Increase muscle strength, because of the positive relationship between strength and power.
LENGTH: 4 weeks
INTENSITY: Select a resistance that allows for completion of the full number of required repetitions on *each* set prior to increasing resistance.
PACE: Perform total-body lifts explosively. For all other exercises, lift in 2 seconds and lower in 3 seconds.
REST: 2:00 between all sets and exercises
SETS/REPS:
- Jan 13–Jan 19: TB=3x3, CL=3x7, AL=3x7
- Jan 20–Jan 26: TB=4x6, CL=4x9, AL=3x9
- Jan 27–Feb 2: TB=4x3, CL=4x7, AL=3x7
- Feb 3–Feb 9: TB=4x6, CL=4x9, AL=3x9

	Week 1 THURS	Week 2 MON	Week 3 THURS	Week 4 MON
TOTAL BODY Squat Clean (FLR) TB WT Lifted	3x3 ___	4x6 ___	4x3 ___	4x6 ___
CHEST Bench Press CL WT Lifted	3x7 ___	4x9 ___	4x7 ___	4x9 ___
Bar/Keg/Log Incline CL WT Lifted	3x7 ___	4x9 ___	4x7 ___	4x9 ___
TRUNK MB Circles WT Lifted	3x20 ___	3x20 ___	3x20 ___	3x20 ___
Leg Throws WT Lifted	3x20 ___	3x20 ___	3x20 ___	3x20 ___
WT Glute Ham WT Lifted	3x10 ___	3x10 ___	3x10 ___	3x10 ___
SHOULDERS Upright Row CL WT Lifted	3x7 ___	4x9 ___	4x7 ___	4x9 ___
Squat Plate Raise CL WT Lifted	3x7 ___	4x9 ___	4x7 ___	4x9 ___

Thursday/Monday Workout Regimen

Friday/Tuesday

DATES: Jan 13–Feb 9
CYCLE: Strength I
GOAL: Increase muscle strength, because of the positive relationship between strength and power.
LENGTH: 4 weeks
INTENSITY: Select a resistance that allows for completion of the full number of required repetitions on *each* set prior to increasing resistance.
PACE: Perform total-body lifts explosively. For all other exercises, lift in 2 seconds and lower in 3 seconds.
REST: 2:00 between all sets and exercises
SETS/REPS:

- Jan 13–Jan 19: TB=3x3, CL=3x7, AL=3x7
- Jan 20–Jan 26: TB=4x6, CL=4x9, AL=3x9
- Jan 27–Feb 2: TB=4x3, CL=4x7, AL=3x7
- Feb 3–Feb 9: TB=4x6, CL=4x9, AL=3x9

	Week 1 FRI	Week 2 TUES	Week 3 FRI	Week 4 TUES
TOTAL BODY DB Push Press TB WT Lifted	3x3 ____	4x6 ____	4x3 ____	4x6 ____
LOWER BODY DB Front Squats CL WT Lifted	3x7 ____	4x9 ____	4x7 ____	4x9 ____
DB/Keg/Log SLDL CL WT Lifted (Perform 1 Set Keg/Log)	3x7 ____	3x9 ____	3x7 ____	3x9 ____
Bar/Keg/Log Good Morning CL WT Lifted (Perform 1 Set Keg/Log)	3x7 ____	3x9 ____	3x7 ____	3x9 ____
1x60-Second Stabilization Each Leg	1x60 sec ____	1x60 sec ____	1x60 sec ____	1x60 sec ____
MR Neck MR Flexion/Extension Reps Completed	2x8 ____	2x8 ____	2x8 ____	2x8 ____
MR Training (Prepare for maximum effort in the gym)	See Board	See Board	See Board	See Board

Friday/Tuesday Workout Regimen

Strength Cycle II

OFFENSIVE LINEMEN/TIGHT ENDS

Monday/Thursday
DATES: Feb 10–March 23
CYCLE: Strength II
GOAL: Increase muscle strength, because of the positive relationship between strength and power.
LENGTH: 6 weeks
INTENSITY: Select a resistance that allows for completion of the full number of required repetitions on the first set only prior to increasing resistance.
PACE: Perform total-body lifts explosively. For all other exercises, lift in 2 seconds and lower in 3 seconds.
REST: 2:30 between total-body exercises, 2:00 between all other sets and exercises
SETS/REPS:
- Feb 10–Feb 16: TB=4x5, CL=4x6, AL=3x6
- Feb 17–Feb 23: TB=4x3, CL=4x4, AL=3x6
- Feb 24–March 2: TB=4x5, CL=4x6, AL=3x6
- March 3–March 9: TB=4x3, CL=4x4, AL=3x6
- March 10–March 16: TB=4x5, CL=4x6, AL=3x6
- March 17–March 23: TB=4x3, CL=4x4, AL=3x6

	Week 1 MON	Week 2 THURS	Week 3 MON	Week 4 THURS	Week 5 MON	Week 6 THURS
TOTAL BODY DB Split ALT FT Jerk TB WT Lifted	4x5 ___	4x3 ___	4x5 ___	4x3 ___	4x5 ___	4x3 ___
CHEST DB/Keg/Log Bench CL WT Lifted (Partial First Set)	4x6 ___	4x4 ___	4x6 ___	4x4 ___	4x6 ___	4x4 ___
TRUNK MB Push-Downs Reps Completed	3x15 ___	3x15 ___	3x15 ___	3x15 ___	3x15 ___	3x15 ___
WT Reverse Back Extensions WT Lifted	3x10 ___	3x10 ___	3x10 ___	3x10 ___	3x10 ___	3x10 ___
SHOULDERS DB Upright Row CL WT Lifted	4x6 ___	4x4 ___	4x6 ___	4x4 ___	4x6 ___	4x4 ___
MR Front Raise (1-Leg/Eyes Closed) Reps Completed	2x8 ___	2x8 ___	2x8 ___	2x8 ___	2x8 ___	2x8 ___
BICEPS MR Biceps AL WT Lifted	2x8 ___	2x8 ___	2x8 ___	2x8 ___	2x8 ___	2x8 ___

Monday/Thursday Workout Regimen

Tuesday/Friday
DATES: Feb 10–March 23
CYCLE: Strength II
GOAL: Increase muscle strength, because of the positive relationship between strength and power.
LENGTH: 6 weeks
INTENSITY: Select a resistance that allows for completion of the full number of required repetitions on the *first* set only prior to increasing resistance.
PACE: Perform total-body lifts explosively. For all other exercises, lift in 2 seconds and lower in 3 seconds.
REST: 2:30 between total-body exercises, 2:00 between all other sets and exercises
SETS/REPS:

- Feb 10–Feb 16: TB=4x5, CL=4x6, AL=3x6
- Feb 17–Feb 23: TB=4x3, CL=4x4, AL=3x6
- Feb 24–March 2: TB=4x5, CL=4x6, AL=3x6
- March 3–March 9: TB=4x3, CL=4x4, AL=3x6
- March 10–March 16: TB=4x5, CL=4x6, AL=3x6
- March 17–March 23: TB=4x3, CL=4x4, AL=3x6

	Week 1 TUES	Week 2 FRI	Week 3 TUES	Week 4 FRI	Week 5 TUES	Week 6 FRI
TOTAL BODY Split ALT FT Snatch (FLR) TB WT Lifted	4x5 ____	4x3 ____	4x5 ____	4x3 ____	4x5 ____	4x3 ____
LOWER BODY Squat (Partial First Set) CL WT Lifted	4x6 ____	4x4 ____	4x6 ____	4x4 ____	4x6 ____	4x4 ____
Leg Curl/MR Leg Curl AL WT Lifted	3x6/2x8 ____	3x6/2x8 ____	3x6/2x8 ____	3x6/2x8 ____	3x6/2x8 ____	3x6/2x8 ____
1x60-Second Stabilization Each Leg	1x60 sec ____	1x60 sec ____	1x60 sec ____	1x60 sec ____	1x60 sec ____	1x60 sec ____
TRUNK WT V-Ups/with MB WT Lifted	3x15 ____	3x15 ____	3x15 ____	3x15 ____	3x15 ____	3x15 ____
MR Seated Twists Reps Completed	3x15 ____	3x15 ____	3x15 ____	3x15 ____	3x15 ____	3x15 ____
UPPER BACK Seated Row/PD/T-Bar CL WT Lifted	4x6 ____	4x4 ____	4x6 ____	4x4 ____	4x6 ____	4x4 ____
NECK MR Lateral Flexion Reps Completed	2x8 ____	2x8 ____	2x8 ____	2x8 ____	2x8 ____	2x8 ____

Tuesday/Friday Workout Regimen

Thursday/Monday

DATES: Feb 10–March 23
CYCLE: Strength II
GOAL: Increase muscle strength, because of the positive relationship between strength and power.
LENGTH: 6 weeks
INTENSITY: Select a resistance that allows for completion of the full number of required repetitions on the *first* set only prior to increasing resistance.
PACE: Perform total-body lifts explosively. For all other exercises, lift in 2 seconds and lower in 3 seconds.
REST: 2:30 between total-body exercises, 2:00 between all other sets and exercises
SETS/REPS:

- Feb 10–Feb 16: TB=4x3, CL=4x4, AL=3x6
- Feb 17–Feb 23: TB=4x5, CL=4x6, AL=3x6
- Feb 24–March 2: TB=4x3, CL=4x4, AL=3x6
- March 3–March 9: TB=4x5, CL=4x6, AL=3x6
- March 10–March 16: TB=4x3, CL=4x4, AL=3x6
- March 17–March 23: TB=4x5, CL=4x6, AL=3x6

	Week 1 THURS	Week 2 MON	Week 3 THURS	Week 4 MON	Week 5 THURS	Week 6 MON
TOTAL BODY Squat Cleans (FLR) TB WT Lifted	4x3 ____	4x5 ____	4x3 ____	4x5 ____	4x3 ____	4x5 ____
CHEST Bench Press CL WT Lifted (Partial First Set)	4x4 ____	4x6 ____	4x4 ____	4x6 ____	4x4 ____	4x6 ____
Bar/Keg/Log Incline CL Reps Completed (Partial First Set)	4x4 ____	4x6 ____	4x4 ____	4x6 ____	4x4 ____	4x6 ____
TRUNK WT Bicycles Reps Completed	3x15 ____	3x15 ____	3x15 ____	3x15 ____	3x15 ____	3x15 ____
WT Reverse Back Extension WT Lifted	3x10 ____	3x10 ____	3x10 ____	3x10 ____	3x10 ____	3x10 ____
SHOULDERS MR Shoulder Press Reps Completed	2x8 ____	2x8 ____	2x8 ____	2x8 ____	2x8 ____	2x8 ____
BICEPS MR Hammer Curl (1-Leg/Eyes Closed) WT Lifted	2x8 ____	2x8 ____	2x8 ____	2x8 ____	2x8 ____	2x8 ____

Thursday/Monday Workout Regimen

Friday/Tuesday

DATES: Feb 10–March 23
CYCLE: Strength II
GOAL: Increase muscle strength, because of the positive relationship between strength and power.
LENGTH: 6 weeks
INTENSITY: Select a resistance that allows for completion of the full number of required repetitions on the *first* set only prior to increasing resistance.
PACE: Perform total-body lifts explosively. For all other exercises, lift in 2 seconds and lower in 3 seconds.
REST: 2:30 between total-body exercises, 2:00 between all other sets and exercises
SETS/REPS:

- Feb 10–Feb 16: TB=4x3, CL=4x4, AL=3x6
- Feb 17–Feb 23: TB=4x5, CL=4x6, AL=3x6
- Feb 24–March 2: TB=4x3, CL=4x4, AL=3x6
- March 3–March 9: TB=4x5, CL=4x6, AL=3x6
- March 10–March 16: TB=4x3, CL=4x4, AL=3x6
- March 17–March 23: TB=4x5, CL=4x6, AL=3x6

	Week 1 FRI	Week 2 TUES	Week 3 FRI	Week 4 TUES	Week 5 FRI	Week 6 TUES
TOTAL BODY DB Split ALT FT Snatch (FLR) TB WT Lifted	4x3 ___	4x5 ___	4x3 ___	4x5 ___	4x3 ___	4x5 ___
LOWER BODY DB/Keg/Log 1-Leg Squat CL WT Lifted (Partial First Set)	4x4 ___	4x6 ___	4x4 ___	4x6 ___	4x4 ___	4x6 ___
DB/Keg/Log Lateral Squat CL WT Lifted (Each Leg)	4x4 ___	4x6 ___	4x4 ___	4x6 ___	4x4 ___	4x6 ___
TRUNK WT Decline Crunch WT Lifted	3x15 ___	3x15 ___	3x15 ___	3x15 ___	3x15 ___	3x15 ___
WT Decline Twist WT Lifted	3x15 ___	3x15 ___	3x15 ___	3x15 ___	3x15 ___	3x15 ___
UPPER BACK DB Upright Row CL WT Lifted (1-Leg/Eyes Closed)	2x8 ___	2x8 ___	2x8 ___	2x8 ___	2x8 ___	2x8 ___
NECK MR Flexion/Extension Reps Completed	2x8 ___	2x8 ___	2x8 ___	2x8 ___	2x8 ___	2x8 ___

Friday/Tuesday Workout Regimen

Spring Practice

DEFENSIVE LINEMEN/LINEBACKERS

Day 1
DATES: March 31–April 27
CYCLE: Spring Practice
GOAL: Increase strength and power during the competitive season.
LENGTH: 4 weeks
INTENSITY: For total-body exercises, select a resistance that allows for completion of the full number of required repetitions on the *first* set only prior to increasing resistance. For timed exercises, reduce the resistance as necessary to maintain the desired speed of movement during each set.
PACE: Perform total-body lifts explosively. Perform timed lifts at a pace that allows for completion of the required number of repetitions in the specified time period.
REST: 3:00 between total-body exercises, 2:30 between all other sets and exercises
SETS/REPS:

- March 31–April 6: TB=3x2, CL=3x3
- April 7–April 13: TB=3x4, CL=3x6
- April 14–April 20: TB=3x2, CL=3x3
- April 21–April 27: TB=3x4, CL=3x6

Day 2
DATES: March 31–April 27
CYCLE: Spring Practice
GOAL: Increase strength and power during the competitive season.
LENGTH: 4 weeks
INTENSITY: For total-body exercises, select a resistance that allows for completion of the full number of required repetitions on the *first* set only prior to increasing resistance. For timed exercises, reduce the resistance as necessary to maintain the desired speed of movement during each set.
PACE: Perform total-body lifts explosively. Perform timed lifts at a pace that allows for completion of the required number of repetitions in the specified time period.
REST: 3:00 between total-body exercises, 2:30 between all other sets and exercises
SETS/REPS:

- March 31–April 6: TB=3x4, TL=3x5@11 sec (2.2)
- April 7–April 13: TB=3x2, TL=3x3@6 sec (2)
- April 14–April 20: TB=3x4, TL=3x511 sec (2.2)
- April 21–April 27: TB=3x2, TL=3x3@6 sec (2)

	Week 1	Week 2	Week 3	Week 4
TOTAL BODY (CHOOSE 1)				
Bar/DB/Tire Squat Cleans (FLR) TB WT Lifted	3x2 ____	3x4 ____	3x2 ____	3x4 ____
Bar/DB Hang Split ALT FT Snatch TB WT Lifted	3x2 ____	3x4 ____	3x2 ____	3x4 ____
Bar/DB Split ALT FT Jerks TB WT Lifted	3x2 ____	3x4 ____	3x2 ____	3x4 ____
LOWER BODY (CHOOSE 2+Stabilization)				
Bar/DB/Keg/Log Squats CL WT Lifted (Partial First Set)	3x3 ____	3x6 ____	3x3 ____	3x6 ____
Bar/DB/Keg/Log Side Lunge CL WT Lifted (Total)	3x3 ____	3x6 ____	3x3 ____	3x6 ____
Leg Curl/MR Leg Curl AL WT Lifted	3x6/2x8 ____	3x6/2x8 ____	3x6/2x8 ____	3x6/2x8 ____
60-Second Stabilization Each Leg	1x60 sec ____	1x60 sec ____	1x60 sec ____	1x60 sec ____
TRUNK (PERFORM BOTH)				
MB Decline Push-Down Reps Completed	3x10 ____	3x10 ____	3x10 ____	3x10 ____
WT Twist 1-Leg Back Extension WT Lifted	3x8 ____	3x8 ____	3x8 ____	3x8 ____
CHEST/SHOULDERS (CHOOSE 2)				
Bar/DB/Keg/Log Incline Press CL WT Lifted (Partial First Set)	3x3 ____	3x6 ____	3x3 ____	3x6 ____
DB ALT Bench Press CL WT Lifted (Total/Partial First Set)	3x3 ____	3x6 ____	3x3 ____	3x6 ____
MR Lateral Raise CL WT Lifted (1-Leg/Eyes Closed)	2x8 ____	2x8 ____	2x8 ____	2x8 ____
NECK				
MR Flexion/Extension Reps Completed	2x8 ____	2x8 ____	2x8 ____	2x8 ____

Day 1 Workout Regimen

	Week 1	Week 2	Week 3	Week 4
TOTAL BODY (CHOOSE 1) DB Split ALT FT ALT Jerks TB WT Lifted	3x4 ____	3x2@85% ____	3x4@75% ____	3x2@85% ____
DB Hang Split ALT FT ALT Snatch TB WT Lifted (On Command)	3x4 ____	3x2@85% ____	3x4@75% ____	3x2@85% ____
DB Hang Squat ALT Clean TB WT Lifted	3x4 ____	3x2@85% ____	3x4@75% ____	3x2@85% ____
LOWER BODY (CHOOSE 2) Bar/DB/Keg/Log Squat CL WT Lifted	3x5@11 sec ____	3x3@6 sec ____	3x5@11 sec ____	3x3@6 sec ____
DB Lateral Step-Up/Lateral Step-Off CL WT Lifted (Total)	3x5 ____	3x3 ____	3x5 ____	3x3 ____
Bar/DB/Keg/Log SLDL CL WT Lifted	3x5@11 sec ____	3x3@6 sec ____	3x5@11 sec ____	3x3@6 sec ____
TRUNK (PERFORM BOTH) MB 1-Leg Speed Rotations WT Lifted	3x10 ____	3x10 ____	3x10 ____	3x10 ____
WT 1-Leg Back Extension WT Lifted	3x8 ____	3x8 ____	3x8 ____	3x8 ____
CHEST/SHOULDERS (CHOOSE 2) Bar/DB/Keg/Log//Bench Press CL WT Lifted	3x5@11 sec ____	3x3@6 sec ____	3x5@11 sec ____	3x3@6 sec ____
Bar/DB/Keg/Log Incline Press CL WT Lifted	3x5@11 sec ____	3x3@6 sec ____	3x5@11 sec ____	3x3@6 sec ____
Bar/DB/Keg/Log Shoulder Press CL WT Lifted	3x5@11 sec ____	3x3@6 sec ____	3x5@11 sec ____	3x3@6 sec ____
NECK MR Lateral Flexion Reps Completed	2x8 ____	2x8 ____	2x8 ____	2x8 ____

Day 2 Workout Regimen

Strength Cycle III

FULLBACKS

Monday/Thursday
DATES: April 28–May 18
CYCLE: Strength III
GOAL: Increase muscle strength, because of the positive relationship between strength and power.
LENGTH: 3 weeks
INTENSITY: Select a resistance that allows for completion of the full number of required repetitions on the *first* set only prior to increasing resistance.
PACE: Perform total-body lifts explosively. For all other exercises, lower in 2 seconds and lift as explosively as possible.
REST: 2:30 between total-body exercises, 2:00 between all other sets and exercises
SETS/REPS:

- April 28–May 4: TB=4x4, CL=4x5, AL=3x6
- May 5–May 11: TB=4x3, CL=4x3, AL=3x6
- May 12–May 18: TB=4x3, CL=4x3, AL=3x6

	Week 1 MON	Week 2 THURS	Week 3 MON
TOTAL BODY Hang Split ALT FT Snatch TB WT Lifted	4x4 ____	4x3 ____	4x3 ____
LOWER BODY Squat (Partial First Set) CL WT Lift	4x5 ____	4x3 ____	4x3 ____
Leg Curl/MR Leg Curl AL WT Lifted	3x6/3x8 ____	3x6/3x8 ____	3x6/3x8 ____
1x60-Second Stabilization Each Leg	1x60 sec ____	1x60 sec ____	1x60 sec ____
Leg Drive Reps Completed	1x5 ____	1x5 ____	1x5 ____
TRUNK MB Push-Downs Reps Completed	3x12 ____	3x12 ____	3x12 ____
WT V-Ups Reps Completed	3x12 ____	3x12 ____	3x12 ____
UPPER BACK Seated Row/PD/T-Bar Row CL WT Lifted	4x5 ____	4x3 ____	4x3 ____
NECK MR Lateral Flexion Reps Completed	2x8 ____	2x8 ____	2x8 ____

Monday/Thursday Workout Regimen

Tuesday/Friday
DATES: April 28–May 18
CYCLE: Strength III
GOAL: Increase muscle strength, because of the positive relationship between strength and power.
LENGTH: 3 weeks
INTENSITY: Select a resistance that allows for completion of the full number of required repetitions on the *first* set only prior to increasing resistance.
PACE: Perform total-body lifts explosively. For all other exercises, lower in 2 seconds and lift as explosively as possible.
REST: 2:30 between total-body exercises, 2:00 between all other sets and exercises
SETS/REPS:

- April 28–May 4: TB=4x4, CL=4x5, AL=3x6
- May 5–May 11: TB=4x3, CL=4x3, AL=3x6
- May 12–May 18: TB=4x3, CL=4x3, AL=3x6

	Week 1 TUES	Week 2 FRI	Week 3 TUES
TOTAL BODY DB Split ALT FT Jerks TB WT Lifted	4x4 ____	4x3 ____	4x3 ____
CHEST DB/Keg/Log Bench (Partial First Set) CL WT Lifted	4x5 ____	4x3 ____	4x3 ____
SHOULDERS DB Front Raise CL WT Lifted	3x6 ____	3x6 ____	3x6 ____
TRUNK MB Kneel Twist Reps Completed WT Reverse Back Extensions WT Lifted	3x12 ____ 3x10 ____	3x12 ____ 3x10 ____	3x12 ____ 3x10 ____
BICEPS MR Biceps (1-Leg/Eyes Closed) WT Lifted	2x8 ____	2x8 ____	2x8 ____
TRICEPS EZ NG Presses AL WT Lifted	3x8 ____	3x8 ____	3x8 ____

Tuesday/Friday Workout Regimen

Thursday/Monday

DATES: April 28–May 18
CYCLE: Strength III
GOAL: Increase muscle strength, because of the positive relationship between strength and power.
LENGTH: 3 weeks
INTENSITY: Select a resistance that allows for completion of the full number of required repetitions on the *first* set only prior to increasing resistance.
PACE: Perform total-body lifts explosively. For all other exercises, lower in 2 seconds and lift as explosively as possible.
REST: 2:30 between total-body exercises, 2:00 between all other sets and exercises
SETS/REPS:

- April 28–May 4: TB=4x3, CL=4x3, AL=3x8
- May 5–May 11: TB=4x4, CL=4x5, AL=3x8
- May 12–May 18: TB=4x3, CL=4x3, AL=3x8

	Week 1 THURS	Week 2 MON	Week 3 THURS
TOTAL BODY DB/Tire Squat Clean (FLR) TB WT Lifted	4x3 ___	4x4 ___	4x3 ___
LOWER BODY DB/Keg/Log 1-Leg Squat CL (Partial First Set) WT Lifted (Each Leg)	4x3 ___	4x5 ___	4x3 ___
DB/Keg/Log Lateral Squat CL WT Lifted (Total)	4x3 ___	4x5 ___	4x3 ___
1x60-Second Stabilization Each Leg	1x60 sec ___	1x60 sec ___	1x60 sec ___
TRUNK WT Partner Twist WT Lifted	3x12 ___	3x12 ___	3x12 ___
MB Twist Push-Down Reps Completed	3x12 ___	3x12 ___	3x12 ___
UPPER BACK DB Row CL WT Lifted	4x3 ___	4x5 ___	4x3 ___
NECK MR Flexion/Extension Reps Completed	2x8 ___	2x8 ___	2x8 ___

Thursday/Monday Workout Regimen

Friday/Tuesday

DATES: April 28–May 18
CYCLE: Strength III
GOAL: Increase muscle strength, because of the positive relationship between strength and power.
LENGTH: 3 weeks
INTENSITY: Select a resistance that allows for completion of the full number of required repetitions on the *first* set only prior to increasing resistance.
PACE: Perform total-body lifts explosively. For all other exercises, lower in 2 seconds and lift as explosively as possible.
REST: 2:30 between total-body exercises, 2:00 between all other sets and exercises
SETS/REPS:

- April 28–May 4: TB=4x3, CL=4x3, AL=3x8
- May 5–May 11: TB=4x4, CL=4x5, AL=3x8
- May 12–May 18: TB=4x3, CL=4x3, AL=3x8

	Week 1 FRI	Week 2 TUES	Week 3 FRI
TOTAL BODY Squat Cleans (FLR) TB WT Lifted	4x3 ___	4x4 ___	4x3 ___
CHEST Bench Press (Perform 1 Set Standing) CL WT Lifted (Partial First Set)	4x3 ___	4x5 ___	4x3 ___
Bar/Keg/Log Incline CL (Partial First Set) Reps Completed	4x3 ___	4x5 ___	4x3 ___
SHOULDERS MR Upright Row (1-Leg/Eyes Closed) WT Lifted	2x8 ___	2x8 ___	2x8 ___
TRUNK MB Decline 1-Arm Throw Reps Completed	3x12 ___	3x12 ___	3x12 ___
WT Reverse Back Extension WT Lifted	3x10 ___	3x10 ___	3x10 ___
BICEPS MR Biceps Curl (1-Leg/Eyes Closed) WT Lifted	2x8 ___	2x8 ___	2x8 ___

Friday/Tuesday Workout Regimen

Strength Cycle IV

OFFENSIVE LINEMEN/TIGHT ENDS

Monday/Thursday
DATES: May 19–June 8
CYCLE: Strength IV
GOAL: Further increase strength, because of the relationship between strength and power.
LENGTH: 3 weeks
INTENSITY: Select a resistance that allows for completion of the full number of required repetitions on the *first* set only prior to increasing resistance.
PACE: Perform total-body lifts explosively. For all other exercises, lower in 2 seconds and lift as explosively as possible.
REST: 2:30 between total-body exercises, 2:00 between all other sets and exercises
SETS/REPS:
- May 19–May 25: TB=4x4, CL=4x4, AL=3x6
- May 26–June 1: TB=4x2, CL=4x2, AL=3x6
- June 2–June 8: TB=4x4, CL=4x4, AL=3x6

	Week 1 MON	Week 2 THURS	Week 3 MON
TOTAL BODY Squat Clean (FLR) TB WT Lifted	4x4 ___	4x2 ___	4x4 ___
LOWER BODY Squats (Partial First Set) CL WT Lifted	4x4 ___	4x2 ___	4x4 ___
DB/Keg/Log 1-Leg SLDL CL WT lifted	3x6 ___	3x6 ___	3x6 ___
60-Second Stabilization Each Leg	1x60 sec ___	1x60 sec ___	1x60 sec ___
Leg Drive Reps Completed	1x5 ___	1x5 ___	1x5 ___
TRUNK 1-Leg Wood Chops Reps Completed	3x10 ___	3x10 ___	3x10 ___
MB Speed Rotations Reps Completed	3x10 ___	3x10 ___	3x10 ___
UPPER BACK DB Shoulder Press CL Reps Completed	4x4 ___	4x2 ___	4x4 ___
NECK MR Flexion/Extension Reps Completed	2x8 ___	2x8 ___	2x8 ___

Monday/Thursday Workout Regimen

Tuesday/Friday

DATES: May 19–June 8
CYCLE: Strength IV
GOAL: Further increase strength, because of the relationship between strength and power.
LENGTH: 3 weeks
INTENSITY: Select a resistance that allows for completion of the full number of required repetitions on the *first* set only prior to increasing resistance.
PACE: Perform total-body lifts explosively. For all other exercises, lower in 2 seconds and lift as explosively as possible.
REST: 2:30 between total-body exercises, 2:00 between all other sets and exercises
SETS/REPS:

- May 19–May 25: TB=4x4, CL=4x4, AL=3x6
- May 26–June 1: TB=4x2, CL=4x2, AL=3x6
- June 2–June 8: TB=4x4, CL=4x4, AL=3x6

	Week 1 TUES	Week 2 FRI	Week 3 TUES
TOTAL BODY DB Hang Split ALT FT ALT Snatch TB WT Lifted	4x4 ___	4x2 ___	4x4 ___
CHEST DB/Keg/Log Incline Press (Partial First Set) CL WT Lifted (Total)	4x4 ___	4x2 ___	4x4 ___
TRUNK MB Stand 1-Leg ALT Reverse Crunch WT Lifted	3x10 ___	3x10 ___	3x10 ___
MB Decline Crunch Throws WT Lifted	3x10 ___	3x10 ___	3x10 ___
WT Twist 1-Leg Glute Ham WT Lifted	3x8 ___	3x8 ___	3x8 ___
SHOULDERS Squat Plate Raise CL WT Lifted	3x10 ___	3x10 ___	3x10 ___
BICEPS MR Hammer Curls (1-Leg/Eyes Closed) Reps Completed	2x8 ___	2x8 ___	2x8 ___

Tuesday/Friday Workout Regimen

Thursday/Monday

DATES: May 19–June 8
CYCLE: Strength IV
GOAL: Further increase strength, because of the relationship between strength and power.
LENGTH: 3 weeks
INTENSITY: Select a resistance that allows for completion of the full number of required repetitions on the *first* set only prior to increasing resistance.
PACE: Perform total-body lifts explosively. For all other exercises, lower in 2 seconds and lift as explosively as possible.
REST: 2:30 between total-body exercises, 2:00 between all other sets and exercises
SETS/REPS:
- May 19–May 25: TB=4x2, CL=4x2, AL=3x6
- May 26–June 1: TB=4x4, CL=4x4, AL=3x6
- June 2–June 8: TB=4x2, CL=4x2, AL=3x6

	Week 1 THURS	Week 2 MON	Week 3 THURS
TOTAL BODY DB/Tire Hang Squat ALT Cleans TB WT Lifted	4x2 ___	4x4 ___	4x2 ___
LOWER BODY DB/Keg/Log 1-Leg Front Squat (Partial First Set) CL WT Lifted (Each Leg)	4x2 ___	4x4 ___	4x2 ___
DB Lateral Step-Up/Lateral Step-Off CL WT Lifted (Total)	4x2 ___	4x4 ___	4x2 ___
TRUNK MB Forward Stand Twist Throw WT Lifted	3x10 ___	3x10 ___	3x10 ___
Keg Twist Lift WT Lifted	3x8 ___	3x8 ___	3x8 ___
UPPER BACK MR Seated Row Reps Completed	2x8 ___	2x8 ___	2x8 ___
NECK MR Lateral Flexion Reps Completed	2x8 ___	2x8 ___	2x8 ___

Thursday/Monday Workout Regimen

Friday/Tuesday

DATES: May 19–June 8
CYCLE: Strength IV
GOAL: Further increase strength, because of the relationship between strength and power.
LENGTH: 3 weeks
INTENSITY: Select a resistance that allows for completion of the full number of required repetitions on the *first* set only prior to increasing resistance.
PACE: Perform total-body lifts explosively. For all other exercises, lower in 2 seconds and lift as explosively as possible.
REST: 2:30 between total-body exercises, 2:00 between all other sets and exercises
SETS/REPS:

- May 19–May 25: TB=4x2, CL=4x2, AL=3x6
- May 26–June 1: TB=4x4, CL=4x4, AL=3x6
- June 2–June 8: TB=4x2, CL=4x2, AL=3x6

	Week 1 FRI	Week 2 TUES	Week 3 FRI
TOTAL BODY Hang Split ALT FT Snatch TB WT Lifted	4x2 ___	4x4 ___	4x2 ___
CHEST Bench (Perform 1-Set Standing) CL WT Lifted (Partial First Set)	4x2 ___	4x4 ___	4x2 ___
NG Bar/Keg/Log Incline (Partial First Set) CL WT Lifted	4x2 ___	4x4 ___	4x2 ___
TRUNK MB Decline 1-Arm Throws Reps Completed	3x10 ___	3x10 ___	3x10 ___
Stand MR Twists WT Lifted	3x10 ___	3x10 ___	3x10 ___
WT 1-Leg Glute Ham WT Lifted	3x8 ___	3x8 ___	3x8 ___
SHOULDERS DB Front Raise CL WT Lifted	3x6 ___	3x6 ___	3x6 ___
BICEPS Any Biceps Exercise AL WT Lifted	3x6 ___	3x6 ___	3x6 ___

Friday/Tuesday Workout Regimen

Programs emphasizing strength, power, and speed put your athletes in a position to dominate their opponents.

Power Cycle I

DEFENSIVE LINEMEN AND LINEBACKERS

Monday/Thursday
DATES: June 9–July 6
CYCLE: Power I
GOAL: Increase muscle power, because of the positive relationship between muscle power and performance.
LENGTH: 4 weeks
INTENSITY: For total-body exercises, select a resistance that allows for completion of the full number of required repetitions on the *first* set only prior to increasing resistance. For timed exercises, reduce the resistance as necessary to maintain the desired speed of movement during each set.
PACE: Perform total-body lifts explosively. Perform timed lifts at a pace that allows for completion of the required number of repetitions in the specified time period.
REST: 3:00 between total-body exercises, 2:30 between all other sets and exercises
SETS/REPS:

- June 9–June 15: TB=5x3, TL=4x5@11 sec (2.2)
- June 16–June 22: TB=5x2, TL=4x3@6 sec (2)
- June 23–June 29: TB=5x3, TL=4x5@11 sec (2.2)
- June 30–July 6: TB=5x2, TL=4x3@6 sec (2)

	Week 1 MON	Week 2 THURS	Week 3 MON	Week 4 THURS
TOTAL BODY Hang Split ALT FT Snatch TB WT Lifted (On Command)	5x3 ___	5x2 ___	5x3 ___	5x2 ___
Split ALT FT Jerk TB WT Lifted	5x3 ___	5x2@90% ___	5x3@80% ___	5x2@90% ___
LOWER BODY Squats CL WT Lifted	1x5 ___	1x3 ___	1x5 ___	1x3 ___
Squats TL WT Lifted	3x5@11 sec ___	3x3@6 sec ___	3x5@11 sec ___	3x3@6 sec ___
Leg Curl TL WT Lifted	3x5@11 sec ___	3x3@6 sec ___	3x5@11 sec ___	3x3@6 sec ___
60-Second Stabilization Each Leg	1x60 sec ___	1x60 sec ___	1x60 sec ___	1x60 sec ___
Leg Drive Reps Completed	1x5 ___	1x5 ___	1x5 ___	1x5 ___
TRUNK MB Off-Center Rotation Throw Reps Completed	3x10 ___	3x10 ___	3x10 ___	3x10 ___
UPPER BACK Towel Grip Seated Row TL WT Lifted	4x5@11 sec ___	4x3@6 sec ___	4x5@11 sec ___	4x3@6 sec ___
NECK MR Flexion/Extension Reps Completed	2x8 ___	2x8 ___	2x8 ___	2x8 ___

Monday/Thursday Workout Regimen

Tuesday/Friday
DATES: June 9–July 6
CYCLE: Power I
GOAL: Increase muscle power, because of the positive relationship between muscle power and performance.
LENGTH: 4 weeks
INTENSITY: For total-body exercises, select a resistance that allows for completion of the full number of required repetitions on the *first* set only prior to increasing resistance. For timed exercises, reduce the resistance as necessary to maintain the desired speed of movement during each set.
PACE: Perform total-body lifts explosively. Perform timed lifts a pace that allows for completion of the required number of repetitions in the specified time period.
REST: 3:00 between total-body exercises, 2:30 between all other sets and exercises
SETS/REPS:

- June 9–June 15: TB=5x3, TL=4x5@11 sec (2.2)
- June 16–June 22: TB=5x2, TL=4x3@6 sec (2)
- June 23–June 29: TB=5x3, TL=4x5@11 sec (2.2)
- June 30–July 6: TB=5x2, TL=4x3@6 sec (2)

	Week 1 TUES	Week 2 FRI	Week 3 TUES	Week 4 FRI
TOTAL BODY DB Split ALT FT Snatch Balance TB WT Lifted	5x3 ___	5x2@90% ___	5x3@80% ___	5x2@90% ___
DB Hang Split ALT FT Snatch TB WT Lifted (On Command)	5x3 ___	5x2 ___	5x3 ___	5x2 ___
CHEST DB/Keg/Log Bench TL WT Lifted (Total)	4x5@11sec ___	4x3@6sec ___	4x5@11sec ___	4x3@6sec ___
TRUNK Sit Fit 1-Leg MB Twists Reps Completed	3x10 ___	3x10 ___	3x10 ___	3x10 ___
WT Reverse Back Extension WT Lifted	3x8 ___	3x8 ___	3x8 ___	3x8 ___
SHOULDERS Squat Plate Raise TL WT Lifted	4x5@11sec ___	4x3@6sec ___	4x5@11sec ___	4x3@6sec ___
BICEPS MR ALT Biceps (1-Leg Eyes Closed) Reps Completed (Each Arm)	2x8 ___	2x8 ___	2x8 ___	2x8 ___

Tuesday/Friday Workout Regimen

Thursday/Monday

DATES: June 9–July 6
CYCLE: Power I
GOAL: Increase muscle power, because of the positive relationship between muscle power and performance.
LENGTH: 4 weeks
INTENSITY: For total-body exercises, select a resistance that allows for completion of the full number of required repetitions on the *first* set only prior to increasing resistance. For timed exercises, reduce the resistance as necessary to maintain the desired speed of movement during each set.
PACE: Perform total-body lifts explosively. Perform timed lifts at a pace that allows for completion of the required number of repetitions in the specified time period.
REST: 3:00 between total-body exercises, 2:30 between all other sets and exercises
SETS/REPS:

- June 9–June 15: TB=5x2, TL=4x3@6 sec (2.2)
- June 16–June 22: TB=5x3, TL=4x5@11 sec (2)
- June 23–June 29: TB=5x2, TL=4x3@6 sec (2.2)
- June 30–July 6: TB=5x4, TL=4x5@11 sec (2)

	Week 1 THURS	Week 2 MON	Week 3 THURS	Week 4 MON
TOTAL BODY DB/Tire Hang Squat ALT Cleans TB WT Lifted	5x2 ___	5x3 ___	5x2 ___	5x3 ___
DB Split ALT FT ALT Jerk TB WT Lifted	5x2 ___	5x3@80% ___	5x2@90% ___	5x3@80% ___
LOWER BODY DB/Keg/Log 1-Leg Squat TL WT Lifted (Each Leg)	4x3@6 sec ___	4x5@11sec ___	4x3@6 sec ___	4x5@11sec ___
DB Lat Step-Up/Crossover Off CL Reps Completed (Total)	4x3 ___	4x6 ___	4x3 ___	4x6 ___
TRUNK WT Toe Touch Reps Completed	3x10 ___	3x10 ___	3x10 ___	3x10 ___
UPPER BACK DB Row TL WT Lifted	4x3@6 sec ___	4x5@11sec ___	4x3@6 sec ___	4x5@11sec ___
NECK MR Lateral Flexion Reps Completed	2x8 ___	2x8 ___	2x8 ___	2x8 ___

Thursday/Monday Workout Regimen

Friday/Tuesday

DATES: June 9–July 6
CYCLE: Power I
GOAL: Increase muscle power, because of the positive relationship between muscle power and performance.
LENGTH: 4 weeks
INTENSITY: For total-body exercises, select a resistance that allows for completion of the full number of required repetitions on the *first* set only prior to increasing resistance. For timed exercises, reduce the resistance as necessary to maintain the desired speed of movement during each set.
PACE: Perform total-body lifts explosively. Perform timed lifts at a pace that allows for completion of the required number of repetitions in the specified time period.
REST: 3:00 between total-body exercises, 2:30 between all other sets and exercises
SETS/REPS:

- June 9–June 15: TB=5x2, TL=4x3@6 sec (2.2)
- June 16–June 22: TB=5x3, TL=4x5@11 sec (2)
- June 23–June 29: TB=5x2, TL=4x3@6 sec (2.2)
- June 30–July 6: TB=5x4, TL=4x5@11 sec (2)

	Week 1 FRI	Week 2 TUES	Week 3 FRI	Week 4 TUES
TOTAL BODY Squat Clean (FLR) TB WT Lifted	5x2 ____	5x3 ____	5x2 ____	5x3 ____
Split ALT FT Snatch Balance TB WT Lifted	5x2 ____	5x3@80% ____	5x2@90% ____	5x3@80% ____
CHEST Bench (Perform 1 Set Standing) CL WT Lifted	1x3 ____	1x5 ____	1x3 ____	1x5 ____
Bench Press TL WT Lifted	3x3@6sec ____	3x5@11sec ____	3x3@6sec ____	3x5@11sec ____
Bar/Keg/Log Incline TL WT Lifted	4x3@6sec ____	4x5@11sec ____	4x3@6sec ____	4x5@11sec ____
TRUNK Sit Fit 1-Leg Ankle Chop Throws WT Lifted	3x10 ____	3x10 ____	3x10 ____	3x10 ____
WT Reverse Back Extension WT Lifted	3x8 ____	3x8 ____	3x8 ____	3x8 ____
BICEPS MR Hammer Curls Reps Completed (1-Leg/Eyes Closed)	2x8 ____	2x8 ____	2x8 ____	2x8 ____

Friday/Tuesday Workout Regimen

Power Cycle II

FULLBACKS

Monday/Thursday
DATES: July 7–July 27
CYCLE: Power II
GOAL: Further increase muscle power, because of the positive relationship between muscle power and performance.
LENGTH: 3 weeks
INTENSITY: For total-body exercises, select a resistance that allows for completion of the full number of required repetitions on the *first* set only prior to increasing resistance. For timed exercises, reduce the resistance as necessary to maintain the desired speed of movement during each set.
PACE: Perform total-body lifts explosively. Perform timed lifts at a pace that allows for completion of the required number of repetitions in the specified time period. For all other exercises, lift in 2 seconds and lower in 3 seconds.
REST: 3:00 between total-body exercises, 2:30 between all other sets and exercises
SETS/REPS:

- July 7–July 13: TB=5x3, TL=4x4@6 sec (1.5)
- July 14–July 20: TB=5x2, TL=4x2@2 sec (1)
- July 21–July 27: TB=5x1, TL=4x2@2 sec (1)

	Week 1 MON	Week 2 THURS	Week 3 MON
TOTAL BODY DB/Tire Squat ALT Cleans (Shin) TB WT Lifted	5x3 ___	5x2 ___	5x1 ___
DB Split ALT FT ALT Jerk TB WT Lifted	5x3 ___	5x2@80% ___	5x1@85% ___
CHEST DB/Keg/Log Incline TL WT Lifted (Total)	4x4@6 sec ___	4x2@2 sec ___	4x2@2 sec ___
TRUNK MB Stand 1-Leg Twist Throws Reps Completed	3x10 ___	3x10 ___	3x10 ___
WT Twist 1-Leg Back Extension WT Lifted	3x8 ___	3x8 ___	3x8 ___
SHOULDERS DB/Keg/Log/Shoulder Press TL WT Lifted	4x4@6 sec ___	4x2@2 sec ___	4x2@2 sec ___
BICEPS MR ALT Biceps (1-Leg Eyes Closed) Reps Completed (Each Arm)	2x8 ___	2x8 ___	2x8 ___

Monday/Thursday Workout Regimen

Tuesday/Friday
DATES: July 7–July 27
CYCLE: Power II
GOAL: Further increase muscle power, because of the positive relationship between muscle power and performance.
LENGTH: 3 weeks
INTENSITY: For total-body exercises, select a resistance that allows for completion of the full number of required repetitions on the *first* set only prior to increasing resistance. For timed exercises, reduce the resistance as necessary to maintain the desired speed of movement during each set.
PACE: Perform total-body lifts explosively. Perform timed lifts at a pace that allows for completion of the required number of repetitions in the specified time period. For all other exercises, lift in 2 seconds and lower in 3 seconds.
REST: 3:00 between total-body exercises, 2:30 between all other sets and exercises
SETS/REPS:

- July 7–July 13: TB=5x3, TL=4x4@6 sec (1.5)
- July 14–July 20: TB=5x2, TL=4x2@2 sec (1)
- July 21–July 27: TB=5x1, TL=4x2@2 sec (1)

	Week 1 TUES	Week 2 FRI	Week 3 TUES
TOTAL BODY Split ALT FT Snatch Balance TB WT Lifted	5x3 ____	5x2@80% ____	5x1@85% ____
Hang Split ALT FT Snatch TB WT Lifted (On Command)	5x3 ____	5x2 ____	5x1 ____
LOWER BODY Squats CL WT Lifted	1x3 ____	1x2 ____	1x2 ____
Squats TL WT Lifted	3x4@6 sec ____	3x2@2 sec ____	3x2@2 sec ____
Bar/Keg/Log RDL TL Reps Completed	4x4@6 sec ____	4x2@2 sec ____	4x2@2 sec ____
60-Second Stabilization Each Leg	1x60 sec ____	1x60 sec ____	1x60 sec ____
Leg Drive Reps Completed	1x5 ____	1x5 ____	1x5 ____
TRUNK MB Decline 2-Ball Twist Reps Completed	3x10 ____	3x10 ____	3x10 ____
UPPER BACK Towel Grip Seated Row TL WT Lifted	4x4@6 sec ____	4x2@2 sec ____	4x2@2 sec ____
NECK MR Flexion/Extension Reps Completed	2x8 ____	2x8 ____	2x8 ____

Tuesday/Friday Workout Regimen

Thursday/Monday

DATES: July 7–July 27
CYCLE: Power II
GOAL: Further increase muscle power, because of the positive relationship between muscle power and performance.
LENGTH: 3 weeks
INTENSITY: For total-body exercises, select a resistance that allows for completion of the full number of required repetitions on the *first* set only prior to increasing resistance. For timed exercises, reduce the resistance as necessary to maintain the desired speed of movement during each set.
PACE: Perform total-body lifts explosively. Perform timed lifts at a pace that allows for completion of the required number of repetitions in the specified time period. For all other exercises, lift in 2 seconds and lower in 3 seconds.
REST: 3:00 between total-body exercises, 2:30 between all other sets and exercises
SETS/REPS:

- July 7–July 13: TB=5x3, TL=4x2@2 sec (1)
- July 14–July 20: TB=5x2, TL=4x4@6 sec (1.5)
- July 21–July 27: TB=5x1, TL=4x2@2 sec (1)

	Week 1 THURS	Week 2 MON	Week 3 THURS
TOTAL BODY Squat Cleans (FLR) TB WT Lifted	5x3 ___	5x2 ___	5x1 ___
Split ALT FT Jerks TB WT Lifted	5x3 ___	5x2@75% ___	5x1@65% ___
UPPER BODY Bench (Perform 1 Set Standing) CL WT Lifted	1x2 ___	1x4 ___	1x2 ___
Bench Press TL WT Lifted	3x2@2 sec ___	3x4@6 sec ___	3x2@2 sec ___
TRUNK MB Decline Push-Down Reps Completed	3x10 ___	3x10 ___	3x10 ___
WT 1-Leg Back Extensions Reps Completed	3x8 ___	3x8 ___	3x8 ___
BICEPS Any Biceps Exercise AL WT Lifted	3x6 ___	3x6 ___	3x6 ___

Thursday/Monday Workout Regimen

Friday/Tuesday
DATES: July 7–July 27
CYCLE: Power II
GOAL: Further increase muscle power, because of the positive relationship between muscle power and performance.
LENGTH: 3 weeks
INTENSITY: For total-body exercises, select a resistance that allows for completion of the full number of required repetitions on the *first* set only prior to increasing resistance. For timed exercises, reduce the resistance as necessary to maintain the desired speed of movement during each set.
PACE: Perform total-body lifts explosively. Perform timed lifts at a pace that allows for completion of the required number of repetitions in the specified time period. For all other exercises, lift in 2 seconds and lower in 3 seconds.
REST: 3:00 between total-body exercises, 2:30 between all other sets and exercises
SETS/REPS:

- July 7–July 13: TB=5x3, TL=4x2@2 sec (1)
- July 14–July 20: TB=5x2, TL=4x4@6 sec (1.5)
- July 21–July 27: TB=5x1, TL=4x2@2 sec (1)

	Week 1 FRI	Week 2 TUES	Week 3 FRI
TOTAL BODY DB Split ALT FT ALT Snatch Balance TB WT Lifted	5x3 ____	5x2@75% ____	5x1@65% ____
DB Hang Split ALT FT ALT Snatch TB WT Lifted (On Command)	5x3 ____	5x2 ____	5x1 ____
LOWER BODY DB/Keg/Log 1-Leg Front Squat TL WT Lifted (Each Leg)	4x2@2 sec ____	4x4@6 sec ____	4x2@2 sec ____
DB Crossover Up/Lateral Step-Off CL WT Lifted (Total)	4x2 ____	4x3 ____	4x2 ____
TRUNK Sit Fit 1-Leg Wood Chop/Twist WT Lifted	3x10 ____	3x10 ____	3x10 ____
Keg Twist Lift WT Lifted	3x10 ____	3x10 ____	3x10 ____
UPPER BACK Pull-Downs TL Reps Completed	4x2@2 sec ____	4x4@6 sec ____	4x2@2 sec ____
NECK MR Lateral Flexion Reps Completed	2x8 ____	2x8 ____	2x8 ____

Friday/Tuesday Workout Regimen

In-Season Cycle I

OFFENSIVE LINEMEN/TIGHT ENDS

Day 1
DATES: July 28–September 7
CYCLE: In-Season I
GOAL: Maintain increases in strength and power during the competitive season.
LENGTH: 6 weeks
INTENSITY: Complete the full number of repetitions in good form on the *first* set only prior to increasing resistance.
PACE: Perform total-body lifts as explosively as possible. For all other exercises, lift in 1.5 seconds and lower in 2 seconds.
REST: 2:00 minutes between total-body exercises, 1:30 between all other exercises
SETS/REPS:

- July 28–Aug 3: TB=3x2, CL=3x3
- Aug 4–Aug 10: TB=3x4, CL=3x5
- Aug 11–Aug 17: TB=3x4, CL=3x5
- Aug 18–Aug 24: TB=3x2, CL=3x3
- Aug 25–Aug 31: TB=3x4, CL=3x5
- Sept 1–Sept 7: TB=3x2, CL=3x3

Day 2
DATES: July 28–Sept 7
CYCLE: In-Season I
GOAL: Maintain increases in strength and power during the competitive season.
LENGTH: 6 weeks
INTENSITY: Complete the full number of repetitions in good form on the *first* set only prior to increasing resistance.
PACE: Perform total-body lifts as explosively as possible. For all other exercises, lift in 1.5 seconds and lower in 2 seconds.
REST: 2:00 minutes between total-body exercises, 1:30 between all other exercises
SETS/REPS:

- July 28–Aug 3: TB=3x4, TL=3x5@8 sec (1.6)
- Aug 4–Aug 10: TB=3x2, TL=3x3@4 sec (1.4)
- Aug 11–Aug 17: TB=3x4, TL=3x5@8 sec (1.6)
- Aug 18–Aug 24: TB=3x2, TL=3x3@4 sec (1.4)
- Aug 25–Aug 31: TB=3x4, TL=3x5@8 sec (1.6)
- Sept 1–Sept 7: TB=3x2, TL=3x3@4 sec (1.4)

	Week 1	Week 2	Week 3	Week 4	Week 5	Week 6
TOTAL BODY (CHOOSE 1)						
Bar/DB/Tire Squat Cleans (FLR) TB WT Lifted	3x2 ____	3x4 ____	3x2 ____	3x4 ____	3x2 ____	3x4 ____
DB Hang Split ALT FT ALT Snatch TB WT Lifted	3x2 ____	3x4 ____	3x2 ____	3x4 ____	3x2 ____	3x4 ____
Bar/DB Split ALT FT Jerks TB WT Lifted	3x2 ____	3x4 ____	3x2 ____	3x4 ____	3x2 ____	3x4 ____
LOWER BODY (CHOOSE 2+Stabilization)						
Bar/DB/Keg/Log Squats CL WT Lifted (Partial First Set)	3x3 ____	3x5 ____	3x3 ____	3x5 ____	3x3 ____	3x5 ____
Bar/DB/Keg/Log Side Lunge CL WT Lifted (Each Leg)	3x3 ____	3x5 ____	3x3 ____	3x5 ____	3x3 ____	3x5 ____
Leg Curl AL WT Lifted	3x5 ____	3x5 ____	3x5 ____	3x5 ____	3x5 ____	3x5 ____
Leg Drive Reps Completed	1x5 ____	1x5 ____	1x5 ____	1x5 ____	1x5 ____	1x5 ____
60-Second Stabilization Each Leg	1x60 sec ____	1x60 sec ____	1x60 sec ____	1x60 sec ____	1x60 sec ____	1x60 sec ____
TRUNK (PERFORM BOTH)						
WT V-Ups WT Lifted	3x10 ____	3x10 ____	3x10 ____	3x10 ____	3x10 ____	3x10 ____
WT Twist Glute Ham WT Lifted	3x8 ____	3x8 ____	3x8 ____	3x8 ____	3x8 ____	3x8 ____
CHEST/SHOULDERS (CHOOSE 2)						
Bar/DB/Keg/Log Bench Press CL WT Lifted	3x3 ____	3x5 ____	3x3 ____	3x5 ____	3x3 ____	3x5 ____
DB ALT Incline Press CL WT Lifted (Total)	3x3 ____	3x5 ____	3x3 ____	3x5 ____	3x3 ____	3x5 ____
DB Lateral Raise CL WT Lifted (1-Leg/Eyes Closed)	3x6 ____	3x6 ____	3x6 ____	3x6 ____	3x6 ____	3x6 ____
NECK MR Flexion/Extension Reps Completed	2x8 ____	2x8 ____	2x8 ____	2x8 ____	2x8 ____	2x8 ____

Day 1 Workout Regimen

	Week 1	Week 2	Week 3	Week 4	Week 5	Week 6
TOTAL BODY (CHOOSE 1)						
Bar/DB Split ALT FT Jerks TB WT Lifted	3x4 ____	3x2@75% ____	3x4@65% ____	3x2@75% ____	3x4@65% ____	3x2@75% ____
DB CMD Hang Split ALT FT ALT Snatch TB WT Lifted	3x4 ____	3x2@75% ____	3x4@65% ____	3x2@75% ____	3x4@65% ____	3x2@75% ____
DB Split ALT FT ALT Jerk TB WT Lifted	3x4 ____	3x2@75% ____	3x4@65% ____	3x2@75% ____	3x4@65% ____	3x2@75% ____
LOWER BODY (CHOOSE 1)						
Bar/DB/Keg/Log Squats TL WT Lifted	3x5@8 sec ____	3x3@4 sec ____	3x5@8 sec ____	3x3@4 sec ____	3x5@8 sec ____	3x3@4 sec ____
DB Lateral Step-Ups/Lateral Step-Off CL WT Lifted (Each Leg)	3x5 ____	3x3 ____	3x5 ____	3x3 ____	3x5 ____	3x3 ____
Bar/DB/Keg SLDL TL WT Lifted	3x5@8 sec ____	3x3@4 sec ____	3x5@8 sec ____	3x3@4 sec ____	3x5@8 sec ____	3x3@4 sec ____
Leg Drive Reps Completed	1x5 ____	1x5 ____	1x5 ____	1x5 ____	1x5 ____	1x5 ____
TRUNK (PERFORM BOTH)						
MB 1-Leg Speed Rotations WT Lifted	3x10 ____	3x10 ____	3x10 ____	3x10 ____	3x10 ____	3x10 ____
WT 1-Leg Back Extension WT Lifted	3x8 ____	3x8 ____	3x8 ____	3x8 ____	3x8 ____	3x8 ____
CHEST/SHOULDERS (CHOOSE 1)						
Bar/DB/Keg/Log Incline Press TL WT Lifted	3x5@8 sec ____	3x3@4 sec ____	3x5@8 sec ____	3x3@4 sec ____	3x5@8 sec ____	3x3@4 sec ____
DB/Keg Incline Press TL WT Lifted	3x5@8 sec ____	3x3@4 sec ____	3x5@8 sec ____	3x3@4 sec ____	3x5@8 sec ____	3x3@4 sec ____
MR Shoulder Press Reps Completed	2x8 ____	2x8 ____	2x8 ____	2x8 ____	2x8 ____	2x8 ____
NECK						
MR Lateral Flexion Reps Completed	2x8 ____	2x8 ____	2x8 ____	2x8 ____	2x8 ____	2x8 ____

Day 2 Workout Regimen

In-Season Cycle II

DEFENSIVE LINE AND LINEBACKERS

Day 1
DATES: Sept 8–Oct 19
CYCLE: In-Season II
GOAL: Maintain increases in strength and power during the competitive season.
LENGTH: 6 weeks
INTENSITY: Complete the full number of repetitions in good form on the *first* set only prior to increasing the resistance.
PACE: Perform total-body lifts as explosively as possible. For all other exercises, lift in 1.5 seconds and lower in 2 seconds.
REST: 2:00 minutes between total-body exercises, 1:30 between all other exercises
SETS/REPS:

- Sept 8–Sept 14: TB=3x5, CL=3x4
- Sept 15–Sept 21: TB=3x3, CL=3x2
- Sept 22–Sept 28: TB=3x5, CL=3x4
- Sept 29–Oct 5: TB=3x3, CL=3x2
- Oct 6–Oct 12: TB=3x5, CL=3x4
- Oct 13–Oct 19: TB=3x3, CL=3x2

Day 2
DATES: Sept 8–Oct 19
CYCLE: In-Season II
GOAL: Maintain increases in strength and power during the competitive season.
LENGTH: 6 weeks
INTENSITY: Complete the full number of repetitions in good form on the *first* set only prior to increasing resistance.
PACE: Perform total-body lifts as explosively as possible. For all other exercises, lift in 1.5 seconds and lower in 2 seconds.
REST: 2:00 minutes between total-body exercises, 1:30 between all other exercises
SETS/REPS:

- Sept 8–Sept 14: TB=3x3, TL=3x2@3 sec (1.5)
- Sept 15–Sept 21: TB=3x5, TL=3x4@7 sec (1.7)
- Sept 22–Sept 28: TB=3x3, TL=3x2@3 sec (1.5)
- Sept 29–Oct 5: TB=3x5, TL=3x4@7 sec (1.7)
- Oct 6–Oct 12: TB=3x3, TL=3x2@3 sec (1.5)
- Oct 13–Oct 19: TB=3x5, TL=3x4@7 sec (1.7)

	Week 1	Week 2	Week 3	Week 4	Week 5	Week 6
TOTAL BODY (CHOOSE 1)						
Bar/DB Hang Split ALT FT Snatch TB WT Lifted	3x5 ____	3x3 ____	3x5 ____	3x3 ____	3x5 ____	3x3 ____
DB Split ALT FT ALT Snatch TB WT Lifted	3x5 ____	3x3 ____	3x5 ____	3x3 ____	3x5 ____	3x3 ____
Bar/DB Split ALT FT Jerks TB WT Lifted	3x5 ____	3x3 ____	3x5 ____	3x3 ____	3x5 ____	3x3 ____
LOWER BODY (CHOOSE 2+Stabilization)						
Bar/DB/Keg/Log Squats CL WT Lift (Partial First Set)	3x4 ____	3x2 ____	3x4 ____	3x2 ____	3x4 ____	3x2 ____
DB Lateral Step-Ups/Lateral Step-Off CL WT Lifted (Total)	3x4 ____	3x2 ____	3x4 ____	3x2 ____	3x4 ____	3x2 ____
Leg Curl/MR Leg Curl AL WT Lifted	3x6/2x8 ____	3x6/2x8 ____	3x6/2x8 ____	3x6/2x8 ____	3x6/2x8 ____	3x6/2x8 ____
60-Second Stabilization Each Leg	1x60 sec ____	1x60 sec ____	1x60 sec ____	1x60 sec ____	1x60 sec ____	1x60 sec ____
TRUNK (PERFORM BOTH)						
MB Stand 1-Leg ALT Reverse Crunch Reps Completed	3x10 ____	3x10 ____	3x10 ____	3x10 ____	3x10 ____	3x10 ____
WT Reverse Back Extension WT Lifted	3x8 ____	3x8 ____	3x8 ____	3x8 ____	3x8 ____	3x8 ____
CHEST/SHOULDERS (CHOOSE 2)						
Bar/DB/Keg/Log Bench Press CL WT Lifted (Partial First Set)	3x4 ____	3x2 ____	3x4 ____	3x2 ____	3x4 ____	3x2 ____
DB ALT Bench CL (Total) WT Lifted (Total/Partial First Set)	3x4 ____	3x2 ____	3x4 ____	3x2 ____	3x4 ____	3x2 ____
Standing Bar Press (Each Arm) WT Lifted (Partial First Set)	3x4 ____	3x2 ____	3x4 ____	3x2 ____	3x4 ____	3x2 ____
NECK						
MR Lateral Flexion Reps Completed	2x8 ____	2x8 ____	2x8 ____	2x8 ____	2x8 ____	2x8 ____

Day 1 Workout Regimen

	Week 1	Week 2	Week 3	Week 4	Week 5	Week 6
TOTAL BODY (CHOOSE 1) Bar/DB/Tire Squat Cleans (FLR) TB WT Lifted	3x3 ____	3x5@65% ____	3x3@75% ____	3x5@65% ____	3x3@75% ____	3x5@65% ____
DB Split ALT FT ALT Jerks TB WT Lifted	3x3 ____	3x5@65% ____	3x3@75% ____	3x5@65% ____	3x3@75% ____	3x5@65% ____
DB CMD Hang Split ALT FT ALT Snatch TB WT Lifted	3x3 ____	3x5@65% ____	3x3@75% ____	3x5@65% ____	3x3@75% ____	3x5@65% ____
LOWER BODY (CHOOSE 1) Bar/DB/Keg 1-Leg Squats TL WT Lifted (Partial First Set)	3x2@3 sec ____	3x4@7 sec ____	3x2@3 sec ____	3x4@7 sec ____	3x2@3 sec ____	3x4@7 sec ____
Bar/DB/Keg/Log Arch Lunge TL WT Lifted (Total)	3x2@3 sec ____	3x4@7 sec ____	3x2@3 sec ____	3x4@7 sec ____	3x2@3 sec ____	3x4@7 sec ____
Keg Lift WT Lifted	3x2@3 sec ____	3x4@7 sec ____	3x2@3 sec ____	3x4@7 sec ____	3x2@3 sec ____	3x4@7 sec ____
TRUNK (PERFORM BOTH) MB Stand 1-Leg Twist Throws Reps Completed	3x10 ____	3x10 ____	3x10 ____	3x10 ____	3x10 ____	3x10 ____
WT Twist Glute Ham WT Lifted	3x8 ____	3x8 ____	3x8 ____	3x8 ____	3x8 ____	3x8 ____
CHEST/SHOULDERS (CHOOSE 1) Bar/DB/Keg/Log Incline Press TL WT Lifted (Partial First Set)	3x2@3 sec ____	3x4@7 sec ____	3x2@3 sec ____	3x4@7 sec ____	3x2@3 sec ____	3x4@7 sec ____
DB ALT Incline Press TL WT Lifted (Total/Partial First Set)	3x2@3 sec ____	3x4@7 sec ____	3x2@3 sec ____	3x4@7 sec ____	3x2@3 sec ____	3x4@7 sec ____
Bar/DB/Log Bench Press TL WT Lift (Partial First Set)	3x2@3 sec ____	3x4@7 sec ____	3x2@3 sec ____	3x4@7 sec ____	3x2@3 sec ____	3x4@7 sec ____
NECK MR Flexion/Extension Reps Completed	2x8 ____	2x8 ____	2x8 ____	2x8 ____	2x8 ____	2x8 ____

Day 2 Workout Regimen

In-Season Cycle III

FULLBACKS

Day 1

DATES: Oct 20–Nov 22
CYCLE: In-Season III
GOAL: Maintain increases in strength and power during the competitive season.
LENGTH: 5 weeks
INTENSITY: Complete the full number of repetitions in good form on the *first* set only prior to increasing resistance.
PACE: Perform total-body lifts performed as explosively as possible. For all other exercises, lift in 1.5 seconds and lower in 2 seconds.
REST: 2:00 minutes between total-body exercises, 1:30 between all other exercises
SETS/REPS:

- Oct 20–Oct 26: TB=3x2, CL=3x3, AL=3x5
- Oct 27–Nov 2: TB=3x4, CL=3x5, AL=3x5
- Nov 3–Nov 9: TB=3x2, CL=3x3, AL=3x5
- Nov 10–Nov 16: TB=3x4, CL=3x5, AL=3x5
- Nov 17–Nov 22: TB=3x2, CL=3x3, AL=3x5

	Week 1	Week 2	Week 3	Week 4	Week 5
TOTAL BODY (CHOOSE 1) Bar/DB/Tire Squat Cleans TB (FLR) WT Lifted	3x2 ___	3x4 ___	3x2 ___	3x4 ___	3x2 ___
DB Split ALT FT ALT Jerks TB WT Lifted	3x2 ___	3x4 ___	3x2 ___	3x4 ___	3x2 ___
LOWER BODY (PERFORM ALL) Bar/DB/Keg/Log Squats CL WT Lifted (Partial First Set)	3x3 ___	3x5 ___	3x3 ___	3x5 ___	3x3 ___
Bar/Keg/Log Side Lunge CL WT Lifted (Total)	3x3 ___	3x5 ___	3x3 ___	3x5 ___	3x3 ___
1x60-Second Stabilization Each Leg	1x60 sec ___	1x60 sec ___	1x60 sec ___	1x60 sec ___	1x60 sec ___
TRUNK (PERFORM BOTH) MB Decline Crunch Throws WT Lifted	3x10 ___	3x10 ___	3x10 ___	3x10 ___	3x10 ___
WT Twist 1-Leg Glute Ham WT Lifted	3x8 ___	3x8 ___	3x8 ___	3x8 ___	3x8 ___
CHEST/SHOULDER (PERFORM BOTH) Bar/DB/Keg/Log Bench Press CL WT Lifted (Partial First Set)	3x3 ___	3x5 ___	3x3 ___	3x5 ___	3x3 ___
Bar/DB/Keg/Log Shoulder Press CL WT (Total) (Partial First Set)	3x3 ___	3x5 ___	3x3 ___	3x5 ___	3x3 ___
NECK MR Flexion/Extension Reps Completed	2x8 ___	2x8 ___	2x8 ___	2x8 ___	2x8 ___

Day 1 Workout Regimen

Day 2

DATES: Oct 20–Nov 22
CYCLE: In-Season III
GOAL: Maintain increases in strength and power during the competitive season.
LENGTH: 5 weeks
INTENSITY: Complete the full number of repetitions in good form on the *first* set only prior to increasing the resistance.
PACE: Perform total-body lifts performed as explosively as possible. For all other exercises, lift in 1.5 seconds and lower in 2 seconds.
REST: 2:00 minutes between total-body exercises, 1:30 between all other exercises
SETS/REPS:

- Oct 20–Oct 26: TB=3x4, CL=3x5@6 sec (1.2)
- Oct 27–Nov 2: TB=3x2, CL=3x3@4 sec (1.4)
- Nov 3–Nov 9: TB=3x4, CL=3x56 sec (1.2)
- Nov 10–Nov 16: TB=3x2, CL=3x3@4 sec (1.4)
- Nov 17–Nov 22: TB=3x4, CL=3x56 sec (1.2)

	Week 1	Week 2	Week 3	Week 4	Week 5
TOTAL BODY (CHOOSE 1) Bar/DB Hang Split ALT FT Snatch TB WT Lifted	3x4 ____	3x2@75% ____	3x4@65% ____	3x2@75% ____	3x4@65% ____
DB Hang Split ALT FT ALT Snatch TB WT Lifted	3x4 ____	3x2@75% ____	3x4@65% ____	3x2@75% ____	3x4@65% ____
LOWER BODY (CHOOSE 1) DB/Keg/Log Lunge TL WT Lifted (Total)	3x5@6 sec ____	3x3@4 sec ____	3x5@6 sec ____	3x3@4 sec ____	3x5@6 sec ____
DB/Keg/Log RDL TL WT Lifted	3x5@6 sec ____	3x3@4 sec ____	3x5@6 sec ____	3x3@4 sec ____	3x5@6 sec ____
TRUNK (PERFORM BOTH) Sit Fit 1-Leg MB Twist WT Lifted	3x10 ____	3x10 ____	3x10 ____	3x10 ____	3x10 ____
Wt 1-Leg Back Extension Wt Lifted	3x8 ____	3x8 ____	3x8 ____	3x8 ____	3x8 ____
CHEST/SHOULDERS (CHOOSE 1) Bar/DB/Keg/Log Incline Press TL WT Lifted	3x5@6 sec ____	3x3@4 sec ____	3x5@6 sec ____	3x3@4 sec ____	3x5@6 sec ____
Keg/Log Bent Row TL WT (Total) (Partial First Set)	3x5@6 sec ____	3x3@4 sec ____	3x5@6 sec ____	3x3@4 sec ____	3x5@6 sec ____
NECK MR Lateral Flexion Reps Completed	2x8 ____	2x8 ____	2x8 ____	2x8 ____	2x8 ____

Day 2 Workout Regimen

4

Speed, Agility, and Plyometric Training

With the current emphasis on speed, spreading the field, and attacking downfield, a high-quality speed and agility program is a necessary requirement for every football program.

Although three separate chapters could certainly be written on speed, agility, and plyometric training, these subjects are combined here into one chapter. The reason is simple: you should combine speed, agility, and plyometric (SAP) training into a single workout.

It is essential that you understand that SAP training is as important as resistance training for improving performance. Football is more than a game of strength and power. It is also a game of speed, quickness, and agility (Figure 4-1). If your team is lacking in any one of these areas you are going to have a hard time being competitive.

Figure 4-1. Football is more than a game of power and strength; it is also a game of speed, quickness, and agility.

All football athletes should participate in SAP training twice each week. SAP training can begin in January when you initiate your off-season training program and continue through the duration of the off-season. Split your SAP training into five cycles, starting with very simple, low-intensity drills and gradually increasing the complexity and intensity of the drills as you progress through the training cycles. In other words, when SAP training begins in January you should initiate training with very basic drills, emphasizing great technique and building a base for the more difficult training to follow. As the weeks go by, training intensity should increase and drill selection should become more specific to the sport of football, so that by June and July drill selection is high in both intensity and specificity.

Skill-position athletes can perform resistance training on Monday, Wednesday, and Friday and participate in SAP training on Tuesday and Thursday. Divide training into two sessions, with the offensive backs and wide receivers in one training session and the defensive backs and kickers in the other session. This design allows you to be more sport-specific in your drill selection. For example, offensive backs may perform a "T" drill in which they sprint from cone to cone. You can perform the same drill with your defensive backs, but have them include backpedaling in the drill to more closely mimic what they have to do athletically.

The offensive linemen, tight ends, fullbacks, defensive linemen, and linebackers also should perform SAP training twice per week. This group of athletes can lift on Monday, Tuesday, Thursday, and Friday and perform SAP training on Wednesday and voluntarily on Saturday. It is a testament to the work ethic of your athletes if you get a very strong turnout each Saturday during the off-season to participate in this voluntary SAP training.

As previously mentioned, the concept of specificity is integral to all phases of training. You should also apply this concept to your SAP training (Figure 4-2). Do not select agility or plyometric drills that do not involve movements similar to ones seen in the game of football. Remember, your goal is to improve performance, and improving your athletes' ability to execute sport-specific movement patterns should be emphasized during all training sessions.

Figure 4-2. Just as the concept of specificity is applied in the resistance-training program, it also needs to be applied in the speed, agility, and plyometric training program.

The goal of SAP training is to increase speed, agility, and quickness. None of these goals can be accomplished effectively when training in a fatigued state. Therefore, you should emphasize the importance of adequate rest periods between sets and exercises (Figure 4-3). Remind your players that you expect 100 percent intensity during training, and the only way that can be accomplished is with adequate recovery.

Figure 4-3. Increasing speed, quickness, and agility requires adequate rest between sets and exercises. Do not allow your speed, quickness, and agility training to become another form of endurance training.

When designing your SAP training, divide the drills into plyometric drills and speed-related drills. Then, split the plyometric drills into football-related and speed-related categories. From there, create a "menu" of drills for each training day. This approach allows you to provide variation in drill selection during each six-week training cycle. SAP training is also organized so that the first training day of the week (Tuesday or Wednesday) is structured to emphasize linear movements and the second training day of the week (Thursday or Saturday) emphasizes lateral movement. This design ensures that linear and lateral training receive a similar degree of emphasis, since both are critical to success in the game of football.

Again, when training for agility, emphasize the concept of specificity by having your position coaches provide movement patterns specific to the positions of their athletes (Figure 4-4). Your goal should be to get the athletes more proficient at the movement patterns they will be using during competition, which is obviously advantageous in terms of improving performance. They should perform these position-specific movement patterns twice per week, once as a part of agility training and once as a part of their conditioning program. The drills you use for your athletes in this section should be a reflection of your own offensive and defensive schemes and use your own terminology.

The following examples of SAP training workouts are in sequence so that you can see how the workouts become more demanding as the athletes progress through the training year. You can also see how to modify the volume and intensity of training for your heavier athletes.

Figure 4-4. The more specific your conditioning program is to the actual demands of the sport, the better. As specificity decreases, so does the value of the time spent training.

SKILL-POSITION ATHLETES

Position: Running Backs/Wide Receivers

Dates: Jan 10–Feb 20
General Warm-Up: 5 minutes—jog, stride, jump rope, exercise bike, etc.

Training Day: Tuesday (Linear Emphasis)

Plyometric Football Drills

- Front box jump (22"–36" box)—3x6
- Front cone hops (6 cones)—3x4
- Jump from box (18"–36" box)—3x6
- Rim jumps—3x6
- Standing jump and reach—3x6
- Standing jump over barrier (22"–36")—3x6
- Standing long jump—3x4

Plyometric Speed Drills

- Alternating push-off (10"–18" box)—3x6 (total)
- Backward skipping—4x25 yards
- Jump to box (22"–36" box)—3x6
- Power skipping for height—4x25 yards
- Single-leg push-off (10"–18" box)—3x6

153

Speed Training

- Ankle pops—2x20 yards
- A-skips—2x20 yards
- Double-leg hurdle hops (four 30"+ hurdles)—3x3
- Downhill sprints (3–5 degrees)—3x25 yards
- Wall drills—march—3x10
- Foot fire—2x10 yards
- Wall drills—march—3x10
- Wall drills—singles—3x12

Agility Drills—Tuesday Only (rest for 30 seconds after each drill)

Running Backs
- Pitch path—run right and sprint 15 yards downfield
- Sweep—run right and sprint 15 yards downfield
- Wheel—run right or left and then sprint an additional 15 yards downfield
- Wheel and set down and then sprint an additional 15 yards downfield
- 5 flat—run right or left and then sprint an additional 15 yards downfield
- Seam and then sprint an additional 15 yards downfield
- Cross—run left or right and then sprint 15 yards downfield
- 4 route and sprint 15 yards downfield
- Pitch path—run left and sprint 15 yards downfield
- Sweep—run left and sprint 15 yards downfield

Wide Receivers
- 12-yard post
- 12-yard flag
- 6-yard stutter and go 20 yards
- 6-yard stutter and go and comeback 13–15 yards
- 30-yard zigzag
- 7–8 yard crossing route
- 22-yard crossing flag
- 5-yard hitch
- 30-yard go
- 17-yard and hook

Training Day: Thursday (Lateral Emphasis)

Plyometric Football Drills

- 30-second box (18"–22" box)—3x30 seconds
- Diagonal cone hops (6 cones)—3x4
- Lateral box jump (18"–22" box)—3x6 (total)

- Lateral jump over barrier (12"–18")—3x6 (total)
- Side throw—3x6 (each side)
- Side-to-side ankle hops—3x6
- Lateral long jump—3x4 (each side)

Plyometric Speed Drills

- Carioca with knee drive—3x20 yards each
- Single foot side-to-side ankle hop—3x8 each
- Hip twist ankle hops—3x10 (total)
- Lateral hop over line (quick)—3x12 (total)
- Side skip with big arm swings—3x20 yards each

Speed Training

- Ankle pops—2x20 yards
- A-Skips—2x20 yards
- Foot fire—2x10 yards
- Double-leg hurdle hops (4 30" + hurdles)—3x3
- Downhill sprints (3–5 degrees)—3x25 yards
- Mountain climbers—3x12 (total)

Position: Defensive Backs

Dates: Feb 21–April 3
General Warm-up: 5 minutes—jog, stride, jump rope, exercise bike, etc.

Training Day: Tuesday (Linear Emphasis)

Plyometric Football Drills

- Double-leg hops—5x25 yards
- Front cone hops (4 cones)—3x4
- Jump to box (22"–36" box)—3x8
- Squat jumps (hands behind head)—3x6
- Standing jump over barrier (18"–24")—3x8
- Standing long jump—3x4
- Depth jump (12"–18" box)—3x6
- Incline push-up depth jump—3x8

Plyometric Speed Drills

- Alternating push-off (10"–18" box)—3x6 (total)
- Backward skipping—4x25 yards
- Jump to box (24"–36" box)—3x6

- Moving split squat with cycle—3x6 (each)
- Power skipping for height—4x25 yards
- Single-leg push-off (10"–18" box)—3x6
- Tuck jump with heel kick—3x8
- Tuck jump with knees up—3x8

Speed Training

- Ankle pops—2x20 yards
- A-skip—2x20 yards
- Double-leg hurdle hops (four 30" hurdles)—3x3
- Foot fire—2x10 yards
- Resisted starts—5x15 yards
- Wall drill—singles—3x12 total
- Wall drill—doubles—3x6 each

Agility Drills—Tuesday Only (rest for 30 seconds after each drill)

- Backpedal 5 yards, churn, sprint forward 10 yards at a 45-degree angle to the left
- Backpedal 5 yards, churn, sprint forward 10 yards at a 45-degree angle to the right
- Swivel hips 20 yards
- Backpedal weave 20 yards
- Backpedal 5 yards, turn and sprint 10 yards at a 45-degree angle to your right, plant at a 90-degree angle, and sprint 5 yards
- Backpedal 5 yards, turn and sprint 10 yards at a 45-degree angle to your right, plant at a 90-degree angle, and sprint 5 yards
- Backpedal 10 yards, toe right and sprint back 10 yards, plant and sprint back, and sprint forward 5 yards
- Backpedal 10 yards, toe left and sprint back 10 yards, plant and sprint back, and sprint forward 5 yards
- Backpedal 10 yards, turn 5 yards at a 45-degree angle to your left, quick turn and sprint 5 yards at a 45-degree angle to your right, then sprint 10 yards
- Backpedal 10 yards, turn 5 yards at a 45-degree angle to your right, quick turn and sprint 5 yards at a 45-degree angle to your left, then sprint 10 yards

Training Day: Thursday (Lateral Emphasis)

Plyometric Football Drills

- 30-second box (18"–22" box)—3x30 seconds
- Cone hops with change-of-direction sprint (4 cones)—3x6
- Diagonal cone hops (6 cones)—3x4
- Lateral box jump (22"–30" box)—3x6 (total)
- Side throw—3x6 (each side)

- Side-to-side ankle hops—3x6
- Standing long jump/lateral sprint—3x6

Plyometric Speed Drills

- Carioca with knee drive—3x25 yards (each)
- Lateral straight-leg crossover run—3x25 yards (each)
- Hip twist ankle hop—3x12 (total)
- Lateral hop over line (quick)—3x14
- Lateral shuffle (2 steps)/10-yard sprint—3x6
- Side skip with big arm swings—3x25 yards

Speed Training

- Ankle pops—2x20 yards
- A-skips—2x20 yards
- Downhill sprints (3–5 degrees)—3x25 yards
- Mountain climbers—3x14 (total)
- Straight-leg skips—2x10 yards
- Touchdown strut—2x30 yards

Position: Quarterbacks

Dates: April 4–May 15
General Warm-Up: 5 minutes—jog, stride, jump rope, exercise bike, etc.

Training Day: Tuesday (Linear Emphasis)

Plyometric Football Drills

- Multiple box-to-box jumps (four 24" boxes)—3x4
- Depth jump (12"–18" box) over barrier (24"–36" box)—3x6
- Double-leg hops—5x25 yards
- Incline push-up depth jump—3x10
- Long jump over barrier (12"–16")—3x6
- Power drop—3x10
- Squat jump (hands behind head)—3x6
- Standing jump over barrier (24"–36")—3x8

Plyometric Speed Drills

- Alternating push-off (10"–18" box)—3x12 (total)
- Moving split squat with cycle—3x10
- Power skipping for height—5x25 yards

- Single-leg push-off (10"–18" box)—3x6 (each leg)
- Squat depth jump (10"–18")—3x10
- Stadium hops—3x10 (total)
- Standing long jump with 10-yard sprint—3x8
- Tuck jump with heel kick—3x8
- Tuck jump with knees up—3x8

Speed Training

- Alternating bounds—2x30 yards
- A-skip—2x20 yards
- Double-leg hurdle hops (four 30"+ hurdles)—3x3
- Long skip (power skip for distance)—2x30 yards
- Single-leg bounds—3x4 each
- Wall drill—doubles—3x6 each
- Wall drill—triples—3x8 total

Agility Drills—Tuesday Only (rest for 30 seconds after each drill)

Note that for certain positions, the agility drills include actual plays used in the offense. This list provides examples of this type of drill. For example, to run the first exercise listed the quarterback takes the steps taken in "play #1." Substitute plays from your playbook into this sequence.

- Sprint out right: Take play #1 steps, attack the line of scrimmage, and sprint 15 yards downfield
- Sprint out left: Take play #2 steps, attack the line of scrimmage, sprint 15 yards downfield
- Lead option steps: Reverse pivot (play #3 or #4), attack the line of scrimmage, and sprint 15 yards downfield
- Inside veer steps: Take 4-step inside veer steps (play #5 or #6 pathway). Accelerate on the fourth step, attack the line of scrimmage, and sprint 15 yards
- Midline steps: Take 4-step midline steps (steps #7 or #8). Accelerate in the "C" gap and sprint 15 yards downfield
- Bootleg steps: Take bootleg steps (play #9 or #10 speed boot) and attack the line of scrimmage. Sprint 15 yards downfield
- 11 steps: Take play #11 steps and accelerate 15 yards downfield
- 12 steps: Take play #12 steps and accelerate 15 yards downfield
- 13 steps: Take play #13 steps and accelerate 15 yards downfield
- 14 steps: Take play #14 steps and accelerate 15 yards downfield

Training Day: Thursday (Lateral Emphasis)

Plyometric Football Drills

- Cone hops/change-of-direction sprint (4 cones)—3x8
- Lateral box jump (18"–22" box)—3x6 (total)
- Lateral cone hops (5 cones)—3x8
- Lateral jump over barrier (12"–18")—3x8 (each)
- Lateral jump with single leg—3x8
- Lateral long jump/forward 10-yard sprint—3x6
- Side throw—3x6 (each side)
- Standing long jump/lateral sprint—3x6 (total)

Plyometric Speed Drills

- Carioca with knee drive—4x25 yards (each)
- Lateral A-skip—3x10 yards (each)
- Lateral crossover run—3x25 yards (each)
- Lateral hop over line (quick)—3x14 (total)
- Lateral shuffle (2 steps) to 10-yard sprint—3x6
- Side skip with big arm swings—3x25 yards
- Single-foot side-to-side ankle hops—3x6

Speed Training

- Alternating bounds—2x30 yards
- Ankle pops—2x20 yards
- Backward strides—3x25 yards
- Downhill sprints (3–5 degrees)—3x25 yards
- Mountain climbers—3x14 (total)
- Straight-leg skips—2x15 yards
- Touchdown strut—3x30 yards

Position: Kickers

Dates: May 16–June 26
General Warm-Up: 5 minutes—jog, stride, jump rope, exercise bike, etc.

Training Day: Tuesday (Linear Emphasis)

Plyometric Football Drills

- Barrier/hurdle hops (four 30"+ hurdles)—3x4
- Depth jump (12"–18" box) over barrier (24"–36")—3x10

- Double-leg hops—6x25 yards
- Incline push-up depth jump—3x10
- Jump to box (24"–36" box)—3x8
- Long jump over barrier (12"–16")—3x6
- Power drop—3x10
- Pyramiding box hops (12"–36")—3x10
- Squat jump (hands behind head)—3x8
- Standing jump over barrier (18"–22")—3x8

Plyometric Speed Drills

- Alternating push-off (10"–18" box)—3x12 (total)
- Moving split squat with cycle—3x10
- Power skipping for height—5x25 yards
- Single-leg push-off (10"–18" box)—3x6
- Single-leg depth jump (10"–12" box)—3x4
- Squat depth jump (10"–18" box)—3x10
- Stadium hops—3x10 (total)
- Standing long jump with 10-yard sprint—3x8
- Tuck jump with heel kick—3x8
- Tuck jump with knees up—3x8

Speed Training

- A-skip—2x20 yards
- Double-leg hurdle hops (four 30"+ hurdles)—3x3
- Long skip (power skip for distance)—2x30 yards
- Mountain climbers—3x14
- Single-leg bounds—3x4 each
- Wall drill—triples—3x8 total
- Wall drill—rapid fire—3x5

Agility Drills—Tuesday Only (rest for 30 seconds after each drill)

- Backpedal 10 yards and return to the starting point on a sprint
- Backpedal 10 yards and return at a 45-degree angle to the right
- Backpedal 10 yards and return at a 45-degree angle to the left
- Backpedal 10 yards and then open up over the left shoulder and sprint 15 yards downfield
- Backpedal 10 yards and then open up over the right shoulder and sprint 15 yards downfield
- Backpedal 10 yards and then slide laterally 5 yards to the right
- Backpedal 10 yards and then slide laterally 5 yards to the left

- Backpedal 10 yards, slide laterally 5 yards to the right, then open up over the right shoulder and sprint 15 yards downfield
- Backpedal 10 yards, slide laterally 5 yards to the left, then open up over the left shoulder and sprint 15 yards downfield
- Backpedal 10 yards and then turn and sprint 30 yards downfield

Training Day: Thursday (Lateral Emphasis)

Plyometric Football Drills

- Cone hops/change of direction sprint (4 cones)—3x10
- Lateral box jump (18"–22" box)—3x12 (total)
- Lateral cone hops (5 cones)—3x10
- Lateral jump over barrier (12"–18")—3x10
- Lateral jump with single leg—3x10
- Zigzag drill—3x15 yards
- Side throw—3x6 (each side)
- Standing long jump/lateral sprint—3x6 (total)

Plyometric Speed Drills

- Carioca with knee drive—4x25 yards (each)
- Lateral A-skip—3x10 yards (each)
- Lateral crossover run—3x25 yards (each)
- Lateral hop over line (quick)—3x14 (total)
- Lateral shuffle (2–3 steps) to 10-yard sprint—3x6
- Side skip with big arm swings—3x25 yards (each)
- Single foot side-to-side ankle hops—3x6 (each)
- 5 yard/10-yard/5-yard shuttle—3x2 (each)

Speed Training

- Ankle pops—2x20 yards
- Backward strides—3x25 yards
- Downhill sprints (3–5 degrees)—3x25 yards
- Mountain climbers—3x14 (total)
- Straight-leg skips—3x15 yards
- Touchdown strut—4x30 yards
- Uphill or resisted starts—5x15

Position: Running Backs/Wide Receivers

Dates: June 27–July 31
General Warm-Up: 5 minutes—jog, stride, jump rope, exercise bike, etc.

Training Day: Tuesday (Linear Emphasis)

Plyometric Football Drills

- Barrier/hurdle hops (four 30"+ hurdles)—3x4
- Depth jump (12"–18" box) over barrier (24"–36")—3x10
- Double-leg hops—6x25 yards
- Incline push-up depth jump—3x10
- Jump to box (24"–36" box)—3x8
- Position stance long jump over barrier (12"–16")—3x6
- Power drop—3x10
- Pyramiding box hops (20"–36")—3x10
- Squat jump (hands behind head)—3x8
- Standing jump over barrier (18"–22")—3x8

Plyometric Speed Drills

- Alternating push-off (10"–18" box)—3x12 (total)
- Moving split squat with cycle—3x10
- Power skipping for height—5x25 yards
- Single-leg push-off (10"–18" box)—3x6 (each leg)
- Single-leg depth jump (10"–12" box)—3x4 (each)
- Squat depth jump (10"–18" box)—3x10
- Stadium hops—3x10 (total)
- Standing long jump with 10-yard sprint—3x8
- Tuck jump with heel kick—3x8
- Tuck jump with knees up—3x8

Speed Training

- A-skip—2x20 yards
- Double-leg hurdle hops (four 30"+ hurdles)—3x3
- Long skip (power skip for distance)—2x30 yards
- Mountain climbers—3x14
- Single-leg bounds—3x4 each
- Wall drill—triples—3x8 total
- Wall drill—rapid fire—3x5 seconds

Agility Drills —Tuesday Only (rest for 30 seconds after each drill)

Running Backs
- Pitch path—run right and sprint 15 yards downfield
- Sweep—run right and sprint 15 yards downfield
- Wheel—run right or left and then sprint an additional 15 yards downfield

- Wheel and set down and then sprint an additional 15 yards downfield
- 5 Flat—run right or left and then sprint an additional 15 yards downfield
- Seam and then sprint an additional 15 yards downfield
- Cross—run left or right and then sprint 15 yards downfield
- 4 route and sprint 15 yards downfield
- Pitch path—run left and sprint 15 yards downfield
- Sweep—run left and sprint 15 yards downfield

Wide Receivers
- 12-yard post
- 12-yard flag
- 6-yard stutter and go 20 yards
- 6-yard stutter and go and comeback 13–15 yards
- 30-yard zigzag
- 7–8 yard crossing route
- 22-yard crossing flag
- 5-yard hitch
- 30-yard go
- 17-yards and hook

Training Day: Thursday (Lateral Emphasis)

Plyometric Football Drills

- Cone hops with change-of-direction sprint (4 cones)—3x10
- Lateral box jump (18"–22" box)—3x12 (total)
- Lateral cone hops (5 cones)—3x10
- Lateral jump over barrier (12"–18")—3x10
- Lateral jump with single leg—3x10
- Zigzag drill—3x15 yards
- Side throw—3x6 (each side)
- Standing long jump/lateral sprint—3x6

Plyometric Speed Drills

- Carioca with knee drive—4x25 yards (each)
- Lateral A-skip—3x10 yards (each)
- Lateral crossover run—3x25 yards (each)
- Lateral hop over line (quick)—3x14 (total)
- Lateral shuffle (2–3 steps) to 10-yard sprint—3x6
- Side skip with big arm swings—3x25 yards (each)
- Single-foot side-to-side ankle hops—3x6 (each)
- 5-yard/10-yard/5-yard shuttle—3x2 (each)

Speed Training

- Ankle pops—2x20 yards
- Backward strides—3x25 yards
- Downhill sprints (3–5 degrees)—3x25 yards
- Mountain climbers—3x14 (total)
- Straight-leg skips—3x15 yards
- Touchdown strut—4x30 yards
- Uphill or resisted starts—5x15

NON-SKILL-POSITION ATHLETES

Position: Defensive Linemen/Linebackers

Dates: Jan 10–Feb 20
General WarmUp: 5 minutes—jog, stride, jump rope, exercise bike, etc.

Training Day: Wednesday (Linear Emphasis)

Plyometric Football Drills

- Front box jump (18"–22" box)—3x4
- Front cone hops (4 cones)—3x4
- Jump from box (18"–22" box)—3x4
- Rim jumps—3x4
- Standing jump and reach—3x45
- Standing jump over barrier (18"–22")—3x4
- Standing long jump—3x4

Plyometric Speed Drills

- Alternating push-off (10"–18" box)—3x6 (total)
- Backward skipping—3x20 yards
- Jump to box (18"–22" box)—3x4
- Power skipping—3x20 yards
- Single-leg push-off (10"–18" box)—3x4

Speed Training

- Ankle pops—2x20 yards
- A-skips—2x20 yards
- Double-leg hurdle hops (three 24"–30" hurdles)—3x3
- Downhill sprints (3–5 degrees)—3x20 yards
- Foot fire—2x5 yards
- Wall drills—march—3x10
- Wall drills—singles—3x12 (total)

Agility Drills—Wednesday Only (rest for 30 seconds after each drill)

Defensive Linemen
- 10-yard shuffle to the right
- 10-yard shuffle to the left
- 5-yard crab
- 10-yard quick-feet carioca left
- 10-yard quick-feet carioca right
- 5-yard/10-yard/5-yard pro agility
- Hoop right
- Hoop left
- 3 yards upfield/turn left/sprint 20 yards
- 3 yards upfield/turn right/sprint 20 yards

Outside Linebackers
- Exit 45 degrees to the right 10 yards and sprint back to the line of scrimmage (LOS)
- Exit 45 degrees to the left 10 yards and sprint back to the LOS
- Exit 45 degrees to the right and sprint 25 yards
- Exit 45 degrees to the left and sprint 25 yards
- Backpedal 10 yards, sprint back to the LOS, exit at a 45-degree angle to the right 10 yards, sprint back to the LOS
- Backpedal 10 yards, sprint back to the LOS, exit at a 45-deg angle to the left 10 yards, sprint back to the LOS
- Backpedal 10 yards, turn and look over the opposite shoulder, sprint 30 yards
- Back pedal 10 yards, turn and look over the opposite shoulder, sprint 30 yards
- Lateral shuffle 10 yards and sprint at a 45-degree angle left 5 yards
- Lateral shuffle 10 yards and sprint at a 45-degree angle right 5 yards

Inside Linebackers
- Backpedal 5 yards, gather, and explode to the cone
- Backpedal 3 yards. On command, open to the right or left. Alternate the direction of the shuffle. Do 3 turns and stay on line for 12 yards
- Backpedal 3 yards. On command, open to the right or left. Alternate the direction of the crossover/run. Do 3 turns and stay on line for 12 yards
- Crossover and work back with width and depth for 5 yards, then flip your hips and gain ground for 5 yards. Change direction 3 times and drive back to the LOS
- Shuffle and work back with width and depth for 5 yards, then flip your hips and gain ground for 5 yards. Change direction 3 times and drive back to the LOS
- Backpedal and, on command, break back to the ball at a 45-degree angle. The backside linebacker should try to gain ground on the frontside linebacker
- Backpedal 5 yards, gather, and explode to cone.
- Backpedal 3 yards. On command, open to the right or left. Alternate the direction of the shuffle. Do 3 turns and stay on line for 12 yards

- Backpedal 3 yards. On command, open to the right or left. Alternate the direction of the crossover/run. Do 3 turns and stay on line for 12 yards
- Crossover and work back with width and depth for 5 yards, then flip your hips and gain ground for 5 yards. Change direction 3 times and drive back to the LOS.

Training Day: Saturday (Lateral Emphasis)

Plyometric Football Drills

- 15-second box (18"–22" box)—3x15 seconds
- Diagonal cone hops (4 cones)—3x4
- Lateral box jump (18"–22" box)—3x4 (total)
- Lateral jump over barrier (12"–18")—3x4 (total)
- Side throw—3x6 (each side)
- Side-to-side ankle hops—3x4 (each side)
- Lateral long jump—3x4 (each side)

Plyometric Speed Drills

- Carioca with knee drive—3x20 yards each
- Single-foot side-to-side ankle hops—3x6 each
- Hip twist ankle hops—3x10 (total)
- Lateral hop over line (quick)—3x12 (total)
- Side skip with big arm swings—3x20 yards each

Speed Training

- Ankle pops—2x20 yards
- A-skips—2x20 yards
- Foot fire—2x5 yards
- Double-leg hurdle hops (four 24"–30" hurdles)—3x3
- Downhill sprints (3–5 degrees)—3x25 yards
- Mountain climbers—3x12 (total)

Position: Fullbacks

Dates: Feb 21–April 3
General Warm-Up: 5 minutes—jog, stride, jump rope, exercise bike, etc.

Training Day: Wednesday (Linear Emphasis)

Plyometric Football Drills

- Double-leg hops—5x25 yards
- Front cone hops (4 cones)—3x4

- Jump to box (22"–36" box)—3x8
- Squat jumps (hands behind head)—3x6
- Standing jump over barrier (18"–36")—3x8
- Standing long jump—3x4
- Depth jump (12"–18" box)—3x6
- Incline push-up depth jump—3x8

Plyometric Speed Drills

- Alternating push-off (10"–18" box)—3x6 (total)
- Backward skipping—3x25 yards
- Jump to box (22"–36" box)—3x6
- Moving split squat with cycle—3x8
- Power skipping for height—4x25
- Single-leg push-off (10"–18" box)—3x6 (each leg)
- Tuck jump with heel kick—3x8
- Tuck jump with knees up—3x8

Speed Training

- Ankle pops—2x20 yards
- A-skip—2x20 yards
- Double-leg hurdle hops (four 30"+ hurdles)—3x3
- Foot fire—2x10 yards
- Resisted starts—5x15 yards
- Wall drill—singles—3x12 total
- Wall drill—doubles—3x6 each

Agility Drills—Wednesday Only (rest for 30 seconds after each drill)

- 1 steps: Take play #1 steps and accelerate 15 yards downfield
- 2 steps: Take play #2 steps and accelerate 15 yards downfield
- 3 steps: Take play #3 steps and accelerate 15 yards downfield
- 4 steps: Take play #4 steps, attack space, and accelerate 15 yards downfield
- 5 steps: Take play #5 steps and accelerate 15 yards downfield
- 6 steps: Take play #6 steps and accelerate 15 yards downfield
- 7 steps: Take play #7 steps and accelerate 15 yards downfield
- 8 steps: Take play #8 steps, attack space, and accelerate 15 yards downfield
- 9 steps: Take play #9 steps and accelerate 15 yards downfield
- 10 steps: Take play #10 steps and accelerate 15 yards downfield

Training Day: Saturday (Lateral Emphasis)

Plyometric Football Drills

- 15-second box (18"–22" box)—3x15 seconds
- Cone hops with change-of-direction sprint (4 cones)—3x6
- Diagonal cone hops (6 cones)—3x4
- Lateral box jump (18"–22" box)—3x6 (total)
- Side throw—3x6 (each side)
- Side-to-side ankle hops—3x6
- Standing long jump/lateral sprint—3x6

Plyometric Speed Drills

- Carioca with knee drive—3x25 yards (each)
- Lateral straight-leg crossover run—3x25 yards
- Hip twist ankle hop—3x12 (total)
- Lateral hop over line (quick)—3x14
- Lateral shuffle (2 steps) to 10-yard sprint—3x6
- Side skip with big arm swings—3x25 yards (each)

Speed Training

- Ankle pops—2x20 yards
- A-skips—2x20 yards
- Downhill sprints (3–5 degrees)—3x25 yards
- Mountain climbers—3x14 (total)
- Straight-leg skips—2x10 yards
- Touchdown strut—2x30 yards

Position: Offensive Linemen/Tight Ends

Dates: April 4–May 15
General Warm-Up: 5 minutes—jog, stride, jump rope, exercise bike, etc

Training Day: Wednesday (Linear Emphasis)

Plyometric Football Drills

- Multiple box-to-box jumps (four 24" boxes)—3x4
- Depth jump (12"–18" box) over barrier (24"–26")—3x3
- Double-leg hops—3x20 yards
- Incline push-up depth jump—3x10
- Jump to box (22"–30" box)—3x4
- Long jump over barrier (12"–16")—3x4
- Power drop—3x10

- Squat jump (hands behind head)—3x6
- Standing jump over barrier (18"–22")—3x8

Plyometric Speed Drills

- Alternating push-off (10"–18" box)—3x12 (total)
- Moving split squat with cycle—3x10
- Power skipping for height—5x25 yards
- Single-leg push-off (10"–18" box)—3x6
- Squat depth jump (10"–12")—3x10
- Stadium hops—3x10 (total)
- Standing long jump with 10-yard sprint—3x8
- Tuck jump with heel kick—3x8
- Tuck jump with knees up—3x8

Speed Training

- Alternating bounds—2x20 yards
- A-skip—2x15 yards
- Double-leg hurdle hops (three 30" hurdles)—3x3
- Long skip (power skip for distance)—2x30 yards
- Single-leg bounds—3x4 each
- Wall drill—doubles—3x6 each
- Wall drill—triples—3x8 total

Agility Drills—Wednesday Only (rest for 30 seconds after each drill)

- Pop release right 3 steps/sprint 10 yards
- Pop release left 3 steps/sprint 10 yards
- Over-and-up step right/sprint upfield 10 yards
- Over-and-up step left/sprint upfield 10 yards
- Drop back right/sprint upfield 10 yards
- Drop back left/sprint upfield 10 yards
- Pull right 5 yards/sprint upfield 10 yards
- Pull left 5 yards/sprint upfield 10 yards
- Bear crawl right 5 yards/sprint upfield 10 yards
- Bear crawl left 5 yards/sprint upfield 10 yards

Training Day: Saturday (Lateral Emphasis)

Plyometric Football Drills

- Cone hops/change-of-direction sprint (4 cones)—3x6
- Lateral box jump (18"–22" box)—3x6 (total)
- Lateral cone hops (5 cones)—3x4

- Lateral jump over barrier (12"–18")—3x4 (each)
- Lateral jump with single leg—3x3
- Lateral long jump/forward 10-yard sprint—3x4
- Side throw—3x6 (each side)
- Standing long jump with lateral sprint—3x4

Plyometric Speed Drills

- Carioca with knee drive—3x25 yards (each)
- Lateral A-skip—3x10 yards (each)
- Lateral crossover run—3x25 yards (each)
- Lateral hop over line (quick)—3x14 (total)
- Lateral shuffle (2–3 steps) to 10-yard sprint—3x6 (total)
- Side skip with big arm swings—3x25 yards (each)
- Single-foot side-to-side ankle hops—3x6 (each)

Speed Training

- A-skip—2x10 yards
- Ankle pops—2x20 yards
- Backward strides—3x20 yards
- Downhill sprints (3–5 degrees)—3x20 yards
- Mountain climbers—3x14 (total)
- Straight-leg skips—2x15 yards
- Touchdown strut—3x20 yards

Position: Defensive Linemen/Linebackers

Dates: May 16–June 26
General Warm-Up: 5 minutes—jog, stride, jump rope, exercise bike, etc.

Training Day: Wednesday (Linear Emphasis)

Plyometric Football Drills

- Multiple box-to-box jumps (four 24" boxes)—3x4
- Depth jump (12"–18" box) over barrier (24"–26")—3x4
- Double-leg hops—4x20 yards
- Incline push-up depth jump—3x10
- Jump to box (22"–30" box)—3x8
- Position stance long jump over barrier (12"–16")—3x4
- Power drop—3x10
- Squat jump (hands behind head)—3x6
- Standing jump over barrier (18"–22")—3x8

Plyometric Speed Drills

- Alternating push-off (10"–18" box)—3x10 (total)
- Moving split squat with cycle—3x10
- Power skipping for height—5x25 yards
- Single-leg push-off (10"–18")—3x6 (each leg)
- Squat depth jump (10"–12" box)—3x10
- Stadium hops—3x10 (total)
- Standing long jump/10-yard sprint—3x8
- Tuck jump with heel kick—3x8
- Tuck jump with knees up—3x8

Speed Training

- Alternating bounds—2x20 yards
- A-skip—2x10 yards
- Double-leg hurdle hops (four 24"–30" hurdles)—3x3
- Long skip (power skip for distance)—2x30 yards
- Single-leg bounds—3x4 each
- Wall drill—doubles—3x4 each
- Wall drill—triples—3x8 total

Agility Drills—Wednesday Only (rest for 30 minutes after each drill)

Defensive Linemen
- 10-yard shuffle to the right
- 10-yard shuffle to the left
- 5-yard crab
- 10-yard quick-feet carioca left
- 10-yard quick-feet carioca right
- 5-yard/10-yard/5-yard pro agility
- Hoop right
- Hoop left
- 3-yards upfield/turn left/sprint 20 yards
- 3-yards upfield/turn right/sprint 20 yards

Outside Linebackers
- Exit 45 degrees to the right 10 yards, sprint back to the LOS
- Exit 45 degrees to the left 10 yards, sprint back to the LOS
- Exit 45 degrees to the right and sprint 25 yards
- Exit 45 degrees to the left and sprint 25 yards
- Backpedal 10 yards, sprint back to the LOS, exit at a 45-degree angle to the right 10 yards, sprint back to the LOS

- Backpedal 10 yards, sprint back to the LOS, exit at a 45-degree angle to the left 10 yards, sprint back to the LOS
- Backpedal 10 yards, turn and look over the opposite shoulder, sprint 30 yards
- Backpedal 10 yards, turn and look over the opposite shoulder, sprint 30 yards
- Lateral shuffle 10 yards and sprint at a 45-degree angle left 5 yards
- Lateral shuffle 10 yards and sprint at a 45-degree angle right 5 yards

Inside Linebackers
- Backpedal 5 yards, gather, and explode to cone.
- Backpedal 3 yards. On command, open to the right or left. Alternate the direction of the shuffle. Do 3 turns and stay on line for 12 yards
- Backpedal 3 yards. On command, open to the right or left. Alternate the direction of the crossover/run. Do 3 turns and stay on line for 12 yards
- Cross over and work back with width and depth for 5 yards, then flip your hips and gain ground for 5 yards. Change direction 3 times and drive back to the LOS
- Shuffle and work back with width and depth for 5 yards, then flip your hips and gain ground for 5 yards. Change direction 3 times and drive back to the LOS
- Backpedal and, on command, break back to the ball at a 45-degree angle. The backside linebacker should try to gain ground on the front side linebacker
- Backpedal 5 yards, gather, and explode to the cone.
- Backpedal 3 yards. On command, open to the right or left. Alternate the direction of the shuffle. Do 3 turns and stay on line for 12 yards
- Backpedal 3 yards. On command, open to the right or left. Alternate the direction of the crossover/run. Do 3 turns and stay on line
- Cross over and work back with width and depth for 5 yards, then flip your hips and gain ground for 5 yards. Change direction 3 times and drive back to the LOS

Training Day: Saturday (Lateral Emphasis)

Plyometric Football Drills

- Cone hops/change-of-direction sprint (4 cones)—3x6
- Lateral box jump (18"–22" box)—3x6 (total)
- Lateral cone hops (5 cones)—3x4
- Lateral jump over barrier (12"–18")—3x4 (each)
- Lateral jump with single leg—3x4
- Lateral long jump/10-yard sprint—3x4
- Side throw—3x6 (each side)

Plyometric Speed Drills

- Carioca with knee drive—3x25 yards (each)
- Lateral straight-leg crossover run—3x25 yards
- Hip twist ankle hop—3x12 (total)

- Lateral hop over line (quick)—3x14
- Lateral shuffle (2 steps) to 10-yard sprint—3x6
- Side skip with big arm swings—3x25 yards (each)

Speed Training

- Alternating bounds—2x20 yards
- A-skip—2x10 yards
- Backward strides—3x20 yards
- Downhill sprints (3–5 degrees)—3x20 yards
- Mountain climbers—3x14 (total)
- Straight-leg skips—2x15 yards
- Touchdown strut—3x30 yards

Position: Fullbacks

Dates: June 27–July 31
General Warm-Up: 5 minutes—jog, stride, jump rope, exercise bike, etc.

Training Day: Wednesday (Linear Emphasis)

Plyometric Football Drills

- Barrier/hurdle hops (four 30"+ hurdles)—3x4
- Depth jump (12"–18" box) over barrier (24"–26")—3x10
- Double-leg hops—6x25 yards
- Incline push-up depth jump—3x10
- Jump to box (22"–30" box)—3x8
- Position stance long jump over barrier (12"–16")—3x6
- Power drop—3x10
- Pyramiding box hops (20"–36")—3x10
- Squat jump (hands behind head)—3x8
- Standing jump over barrier (18"–22")—3x8

Plyometric Speed Drills

- Alternating push-off (10"–18" box)—3x12 (total)
- Moving split squat with cycle—3x10
- Power skipping for height—5x25 yards
- Single-leg push-off (10"–18" box)—3x6 (each leg)
- Single-leg depth jump (10"–12" box)—3x4 (each)
- Squat depth jump—3x10
- Stadium hops—3x10 (total)
- Standing long jump with 10-yard sprint—3x8

- Tuck jump with heel kick—3x8
- Tuck jump with knees up—3x8

Speed Training

- A-skip—2x20 yards
- Double-leg hurdle hops (four 30"+ hurdles)—3x3
- Long skip (power skip for distance)—2x30 yards
- Mountain climbers—3x14
- Single-leg bounds—3x4 each
- Wall drill—triples—3x8 total
- Wall drill—rapid fire—3x5 seconds

Agility Drills—Wednesday Only (rest for 30 seconds after each drill)

- 1 steps: Take play #1 steps and accelerate 15 yards downfield
- 2 steps: Take play #2 steps and accelerate 15 yards downfield
- 3 steps: Take play #3 steps and accelerate 15 yards downfield
- 4 steps: Take play #4 steps, attack space, and accelerate 15 yards downfield
- 5 steps: Take play #5 steps and accelerate 15 yards downfield
- 6 steps: Take play #6 steps and accelerate 15 yards downfield
- 7 steps: Take play #7 steps and accelerate 15 yards downfield
- 8 steps: Take play #8 steps, attack space, and accelerate 15 yards downfield
- 9 steps: Take play #9 steps and accelerate 15 yards downfield
- 10 steps: Take play #10 steps and accelerate 15 yards downfield

Training Day: Saturday (Lateral Emphasis)

Plyometric Football Drills

- Cone hops with change-of-direction sprint (4 cones)—3x10
- Lateral box jump (18"–22" box)—3x12 (total)
- Lateral cone hops (5 cones)—3x10
- Lateral jump over barrier (12"–18")—3x10
- Lateral jump with single leg—3x10
- Zigzag drill—3x15 yards
- Side throw—3x6 (each side)
- Standing long jump/lateral sprint—3x6 (total)

Plyometric Speed Drills

- Carioca with knee drive—4 x25 yards (each)
- Lateral A-skip—3x10 yards (each)
- Lateral crossover run—3x25 yards (each)

- Lateral hop over line (quick)—3x14 (total)
- Lateral shuffle (2 steps) to 10-yard sprint—3x6
- Side skip with big arm swings—3x25 yards (each)
- Single-foot side-to-side ankle hops—3x6 (each)
- 5-yard/10-yard/5-yard shuttle—3x2 (each)

Speed Training

- Ankle pops—2x20 yards
- Backward strides—3x25 yards
- Downhill sprints (3-5 deg)—3x25 yards
- Mountain climbers—3x14 (total)
- Straight-leg skips—3x15 yards
- Touchdown strut—4x30 yards
- Uphill or resisted starts—5x15

5

Conditioning

Superior conditioning can provide a competitive advantage to the football athlete.

It is imperative that your football athletes be in great physical shape if they hope to compete at a high level. Football is an anaerobic activity made up of a series of short-duration, high-intensity work bouts (the average play lasts six to seven seconds), followed by a brief rest period before the ball is put back into play.

The concept of specificity is addressed throughout this book. For example, the value of using dynamic flexibility to increase range of motion is described because it involves stretching using sport-specific positions. In addition, the importance of selecting exercises based on training movements rather than muscle groups is emphasized, as is the importance of selecting drills that mimic the movements of the game when designing speed, agility, and plyometric workouts.

The concept of specificity is also applied in a conditioning program. While football is made up of a series of short-duration sprints, the majority of those sprints do not involve running in a straight line, but instead involve multidirectional movements (think of a linebacker reacting to a play-action fake and then dropping into pass coverage, or a wide receiver running a 10-yard square out and go). To address the need for conditioning specificity, have your position coaches provide a series of sport-specific patterns for your athletes to perform (Figure 5-1). The athletes should complete these sport-specific patterns twice per week, once as a part of agility training (as described in Chapter 4) and once per week intermingled with sprints of varying lengths in the conditioning portion of their training. For example, during the first Thursday workout, the quarterbacks sprint 30 yards, rest for 15 seconds, and then perform play #1. After resting for 15 seconds, the quarterbacks sprint 20 yards and then perform play #2, and so on. This design forces the athletes to adhere to the assigned movement pattern while in a fatigued state, similar to what happens in game situations. You, of course, should insert sport-specific patterns based on the schemes used in your own program.

Figure 5-1. Rather than having athletes perform a series of straight-line sprints as a means to condition, include position-specific movement patterns for them to complete. The more closely the time spent training mimics the demands of the sport, the better.

On the first conditioning day of the week, have your athletes participate in a 300-yard shuttle run, with position-specific speed and rest requirements (Figure 5-2). The 300-yard shuttle run, which is completed over a distance of 25 yards for a total of 12 trips down and back, is also used as a conditioning test for athletes when they report to camp in late summer. To pass the test, athletes must complete the two shuttle runs in the required time and adhere to the position-specific rest times between tests (Table 5-1). The 300-yard shuttle is favored over other conditioning tests because of the nature of the test. The shuttle run requires that the athlete accelerate out of the turns and then reduce speed, stop, and reverse direction, helping to better prepare the athletes for the demands of the sport, as compared to performing a series of straight-ahead sprints.

Figure 5-2. Use the 300-yard shuttle run to test anaerobic endurance. The test involves accelerating, decelerating, and changing direction rather than running straight-line sprints. Preparing for the test better prepares athletes for the demands of fall practice.

Run times for the shuttle run test are as follows:
Offensive linemen, defensive linemen = 64 seconds
Fullbacks, linebackers, tight ends = 60 seconds
Running backs, wide receivers, quarterbacks, defensive backs = 58 seconds

Rest times for the shuttle run test are as follows:
Offensive linemen, defensive linemen = 5:00
Fullbacks, linebackers, tight ends, kickers = 4:45
Running backs, wide receivers, quarterbacks, defensive backs = 4:30

Table 5-1. Shuttle run test run/rest times

As with other forms of training, a good conditioning program is progressive both in volume and intensity. That is, the amount of running required gradually increases and the time allotted to complete that running gradually decreases. For example, during Week 1 the quarterbacks perform one shuttle run in 60 seconds on Tuesday and one series of sprints and pattern runs on Thursday. By Weeks 8 and 9, they are performing three sets of the shuttle run on Tuesdays and four repetitions of the sprint/pattern run complex on Thursdays. Furthermore, the time allowed to complete the shuttle run has been reduced to 56 seconds. The goal is to get the athlete to report to fall practice with a level of conditioning that allows him to participate with a 100-percent level of intensity for the duration of practice.

Tables 5-2 through 5-6 illustrate how the intensity and volume of training is manipulated over the summer to bring the athletes to a peak level of conditioning. The remainder of the chapter presents the conditioning workouts used over the summer to prepare the athletes for the demands of the sport. The skill-position athletes' workouts are shown first, followed by the offensive linemen/tight ends, the defensive linemen/linebackers, and the fullbacks.

Date	Shuttle Run	Sprint/Pattern Run Complex
Week 1	1@60 sec	1 series, rest N/A
Weeks 2–3	1@59 sec	2 series, rest = 10 min between sets
Weeks 4–5	2@58 sec	3 series, rest = 9 min between sets
Weeks 6–7	2@57 sec	4 series, rest = 8 min between sets
Weeks 8–9	3@56 sec	4 series, rest = 7 min between sets

Table 5-2. Quarterbacks, running backs, wide receivers, and defensive backs

Date	Shuttle Run	Sprint/Pattern Run Complex
Week 1	1@65 sec	1 series, rest N/A
Weeks 2–3	1@64 sec	2 series, rest = 10 min between sets
Weeks 4–5	2@63 sec	3 series, rest = 9 min between sets
Weeks 6–7	2@63 sec	4 series, rest = 8 min between sets
Weeks 8–9	3@62 sec	4 series, rest = 7 min between sets

Table 5-3. Offensive linemen

Date	Shuttle Run	Sprint/Pattern Run Complex
Week 1	1@62 sec	1 series, rest N/A
Weeks 2–3	1@61 sec	2 series, rest = 10 min between sets
Weeks 4–5	2@60 sec	3 series, rest = 9 min between sets
Weeks 6–7	2@59 sec	4 series, rest = 8 min between sets
Weeks 8–9	3@58 sec	4 series, rest = 7 min between sets

Table 5-4. Tight ends

Date	Shuttle Run	Sprint/Pattern Run Complex
Week 1	1@64 sec	1 series, rest N/A
Weeks 2–3	1@63 sec	2 series, rest = 10 min between sets
Weeks 4–5	2@62 sec	3 series, rest = 9 min between sets
Weeks 6–7	2@61 sec	4 series, rest = 8 min between sets
Weeks 8–9	3@60 sec	4 series, rest = 7 min between sets

Table 5-5. Defensive linemen

Date	Shuttle Run	Sprint/Pattern Run Complex
Week 1	1@63 sec	1 series, rest N/A
Weeks 2–3	1@62 sec	2 series, rest = 10 min between sets
Weeks 4–5	2@61 sec	3 series, rest = 9 min between sets
Weeks 6–7	2@60 sec	4 series, rest = 8 min between sets
Weeks 8–9	3@59 sec	4 series, rest = 7 min between sets

Table 5-6. Linebackers

Conditioning

Dates: May 23–May 29

Position: Quarterbacks

Note that for certain positions, the agility drills include actual plays or schemes used in the offense. This list provides examples of this type of drill. For example, to run the first exercise listed on Thursday, the quarterback takes the steps he uses in "play #1." Substitute plays and schemes from your playbook as needed.

Tuesday—Perform a 300-yard shuttle run, using 25-yard intervals (1 rep; pace: 60 seconds; rest: N/A)

To complete the following workout, the athlete performs the drill listed in the left-hand column and then rests for the amount of time listed in the right-hand column. For example, here the quarterback sprints 30 yards, rests for 15 seconds, and then performs the sprint-out right drill.

Thursday (1 rep; complete the workout with 100 percent intensity)

	Rest
• Sprint 30 yards	15 sec
• Sprint-out right: Take play #1 steps, attack the line of scrimmage, and follow the pathway of the ball 15 yards downfield	15 sec
• Sprint 20 yards	15 sec
• Sprint-out left: Take play #2 steps, attack the line of scrimmage, and follow the pathway of ball 15 yards downfield	15 sec
• Sprint 25 yards	15 sec

- Lead-option steps: Reverse pivot (play #3 or #4), attack the line of scrimmage, and sprint 15 yards downfield — 15 sec
- Sprint 7 yards — 15 sec
- Inside-veer steps: Take 4-step inside-veer steps (play #5 or #6). Accelerate on the fourth step, attack the line of scrimmage, and sprint 15 yards. Always plant to make the defender miss. — 40 sec
- Sprint 40 yards — 15 sec
- Midline steps: Take 4-step midline pathway (play #7 or #8). Accelerate in the C gap and sprint 15 yards downfield. Always plant to make the defender miss. — 15 sec
- Sprint 8 yards — 15 sec
- Bootleg steps: Take bootleg steps (play #9 or #10), attack the line of scrimmage, and sprint 15 yards downfield — 40 sec
- Sprint 7 yards
  15 sec
- Take play #11 steps and accelerate 15 yards downfield. — 15 sec
- Sprint 40 yards — 15 sec
- Take play #12 steps and accelerate 15 yards downfield — 40 sec
- Sprint 8 yards — 15 sec
- Take play #13 steps and accelerate 15 yards downfield — 15 sec
- Sprint 14 yards — 15 sec
- Take play #14 steps and accelerate 15 yards downfield — N/A

Dates: May 30–June 5

Position: Running Backs/Wide Receivers

Tuesday—Perform a 300-yard shuttle run, using 25-yard intervals (1 rep; pace: 59 seconds; rest: N/A)

Thursday (1 rep; complete the workout with 100 percent intensity)

Running Backs   Rest
- Sprint 30 yards — 15 sec
- Pitch path—run left or right — 15 sec
- Sprint 20 yards — 15 sec
- Sweep—run left or right — 40 sec
- Sprint 25 yards — 15 sec
- Wheel—run left or right — 15 sec
- Sprint 7 yards — 15 sec
- Wheel and set down—run left or right — 40 sec
- Sprint 40 yards — 15 sec
- 5 flat—run left or right — 15 sec

- Sprint 8 yards | 15 sec
- Seam | 40 sec
- Sprint 7 yards | 15 sec
- Play #81 | 15 sec
- Sprint 40 yards | 15 sec
- Play #91 | 40 sec
- Sprint 8 yards | 15 sec
- Cross—run left or right | 15 sec
- Sprint 14 yards | 15 sec
- 4 route | N/A

Wide Receivers — Rest
- Sprint 30 yards | 15 sec
- Pitch path—run left or right | 15 sec
- Sprint 20 yards | 15 sec
- Sweep—run left or right | 40 sec
- Sprint 25 yards | 15 sec
- Wheel—run left or right | 15 sec
- Sprint 7 yards | 15 sec
- Wheel and set down—run left or right | 40 sec
- Sprint 40 yards | 15 sec
- 5 flat—run left or right | 15 sec
- Sprint 8 yards | 15 sec
- Seam | 40 sec
- Sprint 7 yards | 15 sec
- Play #81 | 15 sec
- Sprint 40 yards | 15 sec
- Play #91 | 40 sec
- Sprint 8 yards | 15 sec
- Cross—run left or right | 15 sec
- Sprint 14 yards | 15 sec
- 4 route | N/A

Dates: June 6–June 12

Position: Defensive Backs

Tuesday—Perform a 300-yard shuttle run, using 25-yard intervals (2 reps; pace: 59 seconds; rest: 5 minutes)

Thursday (2 reps; complete the workout with 100 percent intensity)

Rest
- Sprint 30 yards | 15 sec

- Backpedal 5 yards, plant, and sprint forward 10 yards at a 45-degree angle to the left | 15 sec
- Sprint 20 yards | 15 sec
- Backpedal 5 yards, plant, and sprint forward 10 yards at a 45-degree angle to the right | 40 sec
- Sprint 25 yards | 15 sec
- Swivel hips 20 yards | 15 sec
- Sprint 7 yards | 15 sec
- Shuffle 5 yards, backpedal 5 yards, drive back 5 yards, and turn and sprint 10 yards | 40 sec
- Sprint 40 yards | 15 sec
- Backpedal 5 yards, turn and sprint 10 yards at a 45 degree angle to the right, plant at a 90-degree angle, and sprint 5 yards | 15 sec
- Sprint 8 yards | 15 sec
- Backpedal 5 yards, turn and sprint 10 yards at a 45-degree angle to the right, plant at a 90-degree angle, and sprint 5 yards | 40 sec
- Sprint 7 yards | 15 sec
- Backpedal 10 yards, toe right and sprint back 10 yards, plant and sprint back, and sprint forward 5 yards | 15 sec
- Sprint 40 yards | 15 sec
- Backpedal 10 yards, toe left and sprint back 10 yards, plant and sprint back, and sprint forward 5 yards | 40 sec
- Sprint 8 yards | 15 sec
- Backpedal 10 yards, turn 5 yards at a 45-degree angle to the left, quick turn and sprint 5 yards at a 45-degree angle to your right, and sprint 10 yards | 15 sec
- Sprint 14 yards | 15 sec
- Backpedal 10 yards, turn 5 yards at a 45-degree angle to the right, quick turn and sprint 5 yards at a 45-degree angle to the left, and sprint 10 yards | 10 min

Dates: June 13–June 19

Position: Kickers

Tuesday—Perform a 300-yard shuttle run, using 25-yard intervals (2 reps; pace: 58 seconds; rest: 5 minutes)

Thursday (2 reps: complete the workout with 100 percent intensity)

	Rest
- Sprint 30 yards	15 sec
- Backpedal 10 yards and return to the starting point on a sprint	15 sec

• Sprint 20 yards	15 sec
• Backpedal 10 yards and return at a 45-degree angle to the right	40 sec
• Sprint 25 yards	15 sec
• Backpedal 10 yards and return at a 45-degree angle to left	15 sec
• Sprint 7 yards	15 sec
• Backpedal 10 yards and then open up over the left shoulder and sprint 15 yards downfield	40 sec
• Sprint 40 yards	15 sec
• Backpedal 10 yards and then open up over the right shoulder and sprint 15 yards downfield	15 sec
• Sprint 8 yards	15 sec
• Backpedal 10 yards and then slide laterally 5 yards to the right	40 sec
• Sprint 7 yards	15 sec
• Backpedal 10 yards and then slide laterally 5 yards to the left	15 sec
• Sprint 40 yards	15 sec
• Backpedal 10 yards, slide laterally 5 yards to the right, and then open up over the right shoulder and sprint 15 yards downfield	40 sec
• Sprint 8 yards	15 sec
• Backpedal 10 yards, slide laterally 5 yards to the left, and then open up over the left shoulder and sprint 15 yards downfield	15 sec
• Sprint 14 yards	15 sec
• Backpedal 10 yards and then turn and sprint 30 yards downfield	10 min

Dates: June 20–June 26

Position: Quarterbacks

Tuesday—Perform a 300-yard shuttle run, using 25-yard intervals (2 reps; pace: 58 seconds; rest: 4:45)

Thursday (1 rep; complete the workout with 100 percent intensity)

	Rest
• Sprint 30 yards	15 sec
• Sprint-out right: Take play #1 steps, attack the line of scrimmage, and follow the pathway of the ball 15 yards downfield	15 sec
• Sprint 20 yards	15 sec
• Sprint-out left: Take play #2 steps, attack the line of scrimmage, and follow the pathway of the ball 15 yards downfield	40 sec
• Sprint 25 yards	15 sec
• Lead-option steps: Reverse pivot (play #3 or #4), attack the line of scrimmage, and sprint 15 yards downfield	15 sec
• Sprint 7 yards	15 sec

- Inside-veer steps: Take 4-step inside-veer steps (play #5 or #6). Accelerate on the fourth step, attack the line of scrimmage, and sprint 15 yards. Always plant to make the defender miss. 40 sec
- Sprint 40 yards 15 sec
- Midline steps: Take 4-step midline pathway (play #7 or #8). Accelerate in the C gap and sprint 15 yards downfield. Always plant to make the defender miss. 15 sec
- Sprint 8 yards 15 sec
- Bootleg steps: Take bootleg steps (play #9 or #10), attack the line of scrimmage, and sprint 15 yards downfield 40 sec
- Sprint 7 yards 15 sec
- Take play #11 steps and accelerate 15 yards downfield 15 sec
- Sprint 40 yards 15 sec
- Take play #12 steps and accelerate 15 yards downfield 40 sec
- Sprint 8 yards 15 sec
- Take play #13 steps and accelerate 15 yards downfield 15 sec
- Sprint 14 yards 15 sec
- Take play #14 steps and accelerate 15 yards downfield 9 min

Dates: June 27–July 3

Position: Running Backs/Wide Receivers

Tuesday—Perform a 300-yard shuttle run, using 25-yard intervals (2 reps; pace: 58 seconds; rest: 4:45)

Thursday (3 reps; complete the workout with 100 percent intensity)

Running Backs   Rest
- Sprint 30 yards 15 sec
- Pitch path—run left or right 15 sec
- Sprint 20 yards 15 sec
- Sweep—run left or right 40 sec
- Sprint 25 yards 15 sec
- Wheel—run left or right 15 sec
- Sprint 7 yards 15 sec
- Wheel and set down—run left or right 40 sec
- Sprint 40 yards 15 sec
- 5 flat—run left or right 15 sec
- Sprint 8 yards 15 sec
- Seam 40 sec
- Sprint 7 yards 15 sec
- Play #81 15 sec

• Sprint 40 yards	15 sec
• Play #91	40 sec
• Sprint 8 yards	15 sec
• Cross—run left or right	15 sec
• Sprint 14 yards	15 sec
• 4 route	9 min

Wide Receivers	**Rest**
• Sprint 30 yards	15 sec
• 12-yard post	15 sec
• Sprint 20 yards	15 sec
• 12-yard flag	40 sec
• Sprint 25 yards	15 sec
• 30-yard zigzag	15 sec
• Sprint 7 yards	15 sec
• 7–8 yard crossing route	40 sec
• Sprint 40 yards	15 sec
• 22-yard cross flag	15 sec
• Sprint 8 yards	15 sec
• 8-yard hitch	40 sec
• Sprint 7 yards	15 sec
• 22-yard cross flag	15 sec
• Sprint 40 yards	15 sec
• 8-yard hitch	40 sec
• Sprint 8 yards	15 sec
• 30-yard go	15 sec
• Sprint 14 yards	15 sec
• Sprint 14 yards and come back to 12 yards	9 min

Dates: July 4–July 10

Position: Defensive Backs

Tuesday—Perform a 300-yard shuttle run, using 25-yard intervals (3 reps; pace: 57 seconds; rest: 4:30)

Thursday (4 reps; complete the workout with 100 percent intensity)

	Rest
• Sprint 30 yards	15 sec
• Backpedal 5 yards, plant, and sprint forward 10 yards at a 45-degree angle to the left	15 sec
• Sprint 20 yards	15 sec
• Backpedal 5 yards, plant, and sprint forward 10 yards at a 45-degree angle to the right	40 sec

• Sprint 25 yards	15 sec
• Swivel hips 20 yards	15 sec
• Sprint 7 yards	15 sec
• Shuffle 5 yards, backpedal 5 yards, drive back 5 yards, and turn and sprint 10 yards	40 sec
• Sprint 40 yards	15 sec
• Backpedal 5 yards, turn and sprint 10 yards at a 45-degree angle to the right, plant at a 90-degree angle, and sprint 5 yards	15 sec
• Sprint 40 yards	15 sec
• Backpedal 5 yards, turn and sprint 10 yards at a 45-degree angle to the right, plant at a 90-degree angle, and sprint 5 yards	40 sec
• Sprint 8 yards	15 sec
• Backpedal 5 yards, turn and sprint 10 yards at a 45-degree angle to the right, plant at a 90-degree angle, and sprint 5 yards	15 sec
• Sprint 7 yards	15 sec
• Backpedal 10 yards, toe right and sprint back 10 yards, plant and sprint back, and sprint forward 5 yards	15 sec
• Sprint 40 yards	15 sec
• Backpedal 10 yards, toe left and sprint back 10 yards, plant and sprint back, and sprint forward 5 yards	40 sec
• Sprint 8 yards	15 sec
• Backpedal 10 yards, turn 5 yards at a 45-degree angle to the left, quick turn and sprint 5 yards at a 45-degree angle to the right, and sprint 10 yards	15 sec
• Sprint 14 yards	15 sec
• Backpedal 10 yards, turn 5 yards at a 45-degree angle to the right, quick turn and sprint 5 yards at a 45-degree angle to the left, and sprint 10 yards	8 min

Dates: July 11–July 17

Position: Kickers

Tuesday—Perform a 300-yard shuttle run, using 25-yard intervals (3 reps; pace: 56 seconds; rest: 4:30)

Thursday (4 reps; complete the workout with 100 percent intensity)

	Rest
• Sprint 30 yards	15 sec
• Backpedal 10 yards and return to the starting point on a sprint	15 sec
• Sprint 20 yards	15 sec
• Backpedal 10 yards and return at a 45-degree angle to the right	40 sec
• Sprint 25 yards	15 sec

- Backpedal 10 yards and return at a 45-degree angle to the left   15 sec
- Sprint 7 yards   15 sec
- Backpedal 10 yards and then open up over the left shoulder and sprint 15 yards downfield   40 sec
- Sprint 40 yards   15 sec
- Backpedal 10 yards and then open up over the right shoulder and sprint 15 yards downfield   15 sec
- Sprint 8 yards   15 sec
- Backpedal 10 yards and then slide laterally 5 yards to the right   40 sec
- Sprint 7 yards   15 sec
- Backpedal 10 yards and then slide laterally 5 yards to the left   15 sec
- Sprint 40 yards   15 sec
- Backpedal 10 yards and then slide laterally 5 yards to the right, then open up over the right shoulder and sprint 15 yards downfield   40 sec
- Sprint 8 yards   15 sec
- Backpedal 10 yards and then slide laterally 5 yards to the left, then open up over the left shoulder and sprint 15 yards downfield   15 sec
- Sprint 14 yards   15 sec
- Backpedal 10 yards and then turn and sprint 30 yards downfield   8 min

Dates: July 18–July 31

Position: Quarterbacks

Tuesday—Perform a 300-yard shuttle run, using 25-yard intervals (3 reps; pace: 56 seconds; rest: 4:30)

Thursday (1 rep; complete the workout with 100 percent intensity)

                                                                                             Rest

- Sprint 30 yards   15 sec
- Sprint-out right: Take play #1 steps, attack the line of scrimmage, and follow the pathway of the ball 15 yards downfield   15 sec
- Sprint 20 yards   15 sec
- Sprint-out left: Take play #2 steps, attack the line of scrimmage, and follow pathway of ball   40 sec
- Sprint 25 yards   15 sec
- Lead-option steps: Reverse pivot (play #3 or #4), attack the line of scrimmage, and sprint 15 yards downfield   15 sec
- Sprint 7 yards   15 sec
- Inside-veer steps: Take 4-step inside-veer steps (play #5 or #6). Accelerate on the fourth step, attack the line of scrimmage, and sprint 15 yards. Always plant to make the defender miss.   40 sec

• Sprint 40 yards	15 sec
• Midline steps: Take 4-step midline pathway (play #7 or #8). Accelerate in the C gap and sprint 15 yards downfield. Always plant to make the defender miss.	15 sec
• Sprint 8 yards	15 sec
• Bootleg steps: Take bootleg steps (play #9 or #10), attack line of scrimmage, and sprint 15 yards downfield	40 sec
• Sprint 7 yards	15 sec
• Take play #11 steps and accelerate 15 yards downfield	15 sec
• Sprint 40 yards	15 sec
• Take play #12 steps and accelerate 15 yards downfield	40 sec
• Sprint 8 yards	15 sec
• Take play #13 steps and accelerate 15 yards downfield	15 sec
• Sprint 14 yards	15 sec
• Take play #14 steps and accelerate 15 yards downfield.	7 min

Dates: May 23–May 29

Position: Offensive Linemen (OL)/Tight Ends (TE)

Wednesday—Perform a 300-yard shuttle run, using 25-yard intervals (1 rep; pace: OL 66 seconds, TE 63 seconds; rest: N/A)

Saturday (1 rep; complete the workout with 100 percent intensity)

Offensive Line	**Rest**
• Sprint 8 yards	15 sec
• Pop-release right 3 steps and sprint 10 yards	15 sec
• Sprint 6 yards	15 sec
• Pop-release left 3 steps and sprint 10 yards	40 sec
• Sprint 7 yards	15 sec
• Over-and-up step right and sprint upfield 10 yards	15 sec
• Sprint 20 yards	15 sec
• Over-and-up step left and sprint upfield 10 yards	40 sec
• Sprint 6 yards	15 sec
• Drop back right and sprint upfield 10 yards	15 sec
• Sprint 7 yards	15 sec
• Drop back left and sprint upfield 10 yards	40 sec
• Sprint 8 yards	15 sec
• Pull right 5 yards and sprint upfield 10 yards	15 sec
• Sprint 20 yards	15 sec
• Pull left 5 yards and sprint upfield 10 yards	40 sec
• Sprint 8 yards	15 sec
• Bear crawl right 5 yards and sprint upfield 10 yards	15 sec

- Sprint 6 yards — 15 sec
- Bear crawl left 5 yards and sprint upfield 16 yards — N/A

Tight Ends — Rest
- Sprint 6 yards — 15 sec
- Pop-release right 3 steps and sprint 10 yards — 15 sec
- Sprint 40 yards — 15 sec
- Pop-release left 3 steps and sprint 10 yards — 40 sec
- Sprint 7 yards — 15 sec
- Over and up step right and sprint upfield 10 yards — 15 sec
- Sprint 15 yards — 15 sec
- Over and up step left and sprint upfield 10 yards — 40 sec
- Sprint 10 yards — 15 sec
- Drop back right and sprint upfield 10 yards — 15 sec
- Sprint 18 yards — 15 sec
- Drop back left and sprint upfield 10 yards — 40 sec
- Sprint 8 yards — 15 sec
- Search 12 to 10 two-linebacker scheme — 15 sec
- Sprint 20 yards — 15 sec
- Search 12 to 10 three-linebacker scheme — 40 sec
- Sprint 40 yards — 15 sec
- Flag — 15 sec
- Sprint 10 yards — 15 sec
- Post — N/A

Dates: May 30–June 5

Position: Defensive Linemen (DL)/Linebackers (LB)

Wednesday—Perform a 300-yard shuttle run, using 25-yard intervals (1 rep; pace: DL 63 seconds, LB 62 seconds; rest: N/A)

Saturday (1 rep; complete the workout with 100 percent intensity)

Defensive Linemen — Rest
- Sprint 8 yards — 15 sec
- 10-yard shuffle to the right — 15 sec
- Sprint 8 yards — 15 sec
- 10-yard shuffle to the left — 40 sec
- Sprint 24 yards — 15 sec
- 1–2 steps upfield and take on a trap block from the right — 15 sec
- Sprint 10 yards — 15 sec
- 1–2 steps upfield and take on a trap block from the left — 40 sec

• Sprint 10 yards	15 sec
• Sprint 3 yards, turn left, and sprint 20 yards	15 sec
• Sprint 10 yards	15 sec
• Sprint 3 yards, turn right, and sprint 20 yards	40 sec
• Sprint 10 yards	15 sec
• Sprint 5 yards, spin left, and sprint 5 yards	15 sec
• Sprint 40 yards	15 sec
• Sprint 5 yards, spin right, and sprint 5 yards	40 sec
• Sprint 8 yards	15 sec
• Hoop right	15 sec
• Sprint 24 yards	15 sec
• Hoop left	N/A

Outside Linebackers	**Rest**
• Sprint 15 yards	15 sec
• Exit 45 degrees to the right 10 yards and sprint back to the line of scrimmage (LOS)	15 sec
• Sprint 8 yards	15 sec
• Exit 45 degrees to the left 10 yards and sprint back to the LOS	40 sec
• Sprint 11 yards	15 sec
• Exit 45 degrees to the right and sprint 25 yards	15 sec
• Sprint 8 yards	15 sec
• Exit 45 degrees to the left and sprint 25 yards	40 sec
• Sprint 10 yards	15 sec
• Backpedal 10 yards, sprint back to the LOS, and exit at 45 degrees	15 sec
• Sprint 25 yards	15 sec
• Backpedal 10 yards, sprint back to the LOS, and exit at 45 degrees	40 sec
• Sprint 8 yards	15 sec
• Backpedal 10 yards, turn right, and look over the opposite shoulder	15 sec
• Sprint 30 yards	15 sec
• Backpedal 10 yards, turn left, and look over the opposite shoulder	40 sec
• Sprint 8 yards	15 sec
• Lateral shuffle 10 yards and sprint at a 45-degree angle left 5 yards	15 sec
• Sprint 40 yards	15 sec
• Lateral shuffle 10 yards and sprint at a 45-degree angle right 5 yards	N/A

Inside Linebackers	**Rest**
• Sprint 15 yards	15 sec
• Backpedal 5 yards, gather, and explode to the cone	15 sec
• Sprint 8 yards	15 sec

- Backpedal 3 yards and, on command, open to the right. Alternate the direction of the shuffle. Do 3 turns and stay on line for 12 yards.   40 sec
- Sprint 11 yards   15 sec
- Backpedal 3 yards and, on command, open to the right or left. Alternate directions of the crossover/run. Do 3 turns and stay on line for 12 yards. 15 sec
- Sprint 8 yards   15 sec
- Crossover and work back with width and depth for 5 yards, then flip your hips and gain ground for 5 yards   40 sec
- Sprint 10 yards   15 sec
- Shuffle and work back with width and depth for 5 yards, then flip your hips and gain ground for 5 yards   15 sec
- Sprint 25 yards   15 sec
- Backpedal and, on command, break back to the ball at a 45-degree angle   40 sec
- Sprint 8 yards   15 sec
- Backpedal 5 yards, gather, and explode to the cone   15 sec
- Sprint 30 yards   15 sec
- Backpedal 3 yards and, on command, open to the right. Alternate the direction of the shuffle. Do 3 turns and stay on line for 12 yards   40 sec
- Sprint 8 yards   15 sec
- Backpedal 3 yards and, on command, open to the right or left. Alternate the direction of the crossover/run. Do 3 turns and stay on line for 12 yards.   15 sec
- Sprint 40 yards   15 sec
- Crossover and work back with width and depth for 5 yards, then flip your hips and gain ground for 5 yards   N/A

Dates: June 6–June 12

Position: Fullbacks

Wednesday—Perform a 300-yard shuttle run, using 25-yard intervals (2 reps; pace: 62 seconds; rest: 5 minutes)

Saturday (2 reps; complete the workout with 100 percent intensity)

                                                                                                                            Rest
- Sprint 13 yards   15 sec
- Take play #1 steps and accelerate 15 yards downfield   15 sec
- Sprint 8 yards   15 sec
- Take play #2 steps and accelerate 15 yards downfield   40 sec
- Sprint 40 yards   15 sec
- Take play #3 steps and accelerate 15 yards downfield   15 sec

• Sprint 25 yards	15 sec
• Take play #4 steps, attack space, and accelerate 15 yards downfield	40 sec
• Sprint 25 yards	15 sec
• Take play #5 steps and accelerate 15 yards downfield	15 sec
• Sprint 25 yards	15 sec
• Take play #6 steps and accelerate 15 yards downfield	40 sec
• Sprint 25 yards	15 sec
• Take play #7 steps and accelerate 15 yards downfield	15 sec
• Sprint 25 yards	15 sec
• Take play #8 steps, attack space, and accelerate 15 yards downfield	40 sec
• Sprint 40 yards	15 sec
• Take play #9 steps and accelerate 15 yards downfield	15 sec
• Sprint 15 yards	15 sec
• Take play #10 steps and accelerate 15 yards downfield	10 min

Dates: June 13–June 19

Position: Offensive Linemen (OL)/Tight Ends (TE)

Wednesday—Perform a 300-yard shuttle run, using 25-yard intervals (2 reps; pace: OL 64 seconds, TE 61 seconds; rest: 5 minutes)

Saturday (2 reps; complete the workout with 100 percent intensity)

Offensive Linemen

	Rest
• Sprint 8 yards	15 sec
• Pop-release right 3 steps and sprint 10 yards	15 sec
• Sprint 6 yards	15 sec
• Pop-release left 3 steps and sprint 10 yards	40 sec
• Sprint 7 yards	15 sec
• Over-and-up step left and sprint upfield 10 yards	15 sec
• Sprint 20 yards	15 sec
• Over-and-up step left and sprint upfield 10 yards	40 sec
• Sprint 6 yards	15 sec
• Drop back right and sprint upfield 10 yards	15 sec
• Sprint 7 yards	15 sec
• Drop back left and sprint upfield 10 yards	40 sec
• Sprint 8 yards	15 sec
• Pull right 5 yards and sprint upfield 10 yards	15 sec
• Sprint 20 yards	15 sec
• Pull left 5 yards and sprint upfield 10 yards	40 sec
• Sprint 8 yards	15 sec
• Bear crawl right 5 yards and sprint upfield 10 yards	15 sec

• Sprint 6 yards	15 sec
• Bear crawl left 5 yards and sprint upfield 10 yards	10 min

Tight Ends | Rest
• Sprint 6 yards	15 sec
• Pop-release right 3 steps and sprint 10 yards	15 sec
• Sprint 40 yards	15 sec
• Pop-release left 3 steps and sprint 10 yards	40 sec
• Sprint 7 yards	15 sec
• Over-and-up step left and sprint upfield 10 yards	15 sec
• Sprint 15 yards	15 sec
• Over-and-up step left and sprint upfield 10 yards	40 sec
• Sprint 10 yards	15 sec
• Drop back right and sprint upfield 10 yards	15 sec
• Sprint 18 yards	15 sec
• Drop back left and sprint upfield 10 yards	40 sec
• Sprint 8 yards	15 sec
• Search 12 to 10 two-linebacker scheme	15 sec
• Sprint 20 yards	15 sec
• Search 12 to 10 three-linebacker scheme	40 sec
• Sprint 40 yards	15 sec
• Flag	15 sec
• Sprint 10 yards	15 sec
• Post	10 min

Dates: June 20–June 26

Position: Defensive Linemen (DL)/Linebackers (LB)

Wednesday—Perform a 300-yard shuttle run, using 25-yard intervals (2 reps; pace: DL 62 seconds, LB 61 seconds; rest: DL 5 minutes, LB 4:50)

Saturday (3 reps; complete the workout with 100 percent intensity)

Defensive Linemen | Rest
• Sprint 8 yards	15 sec
• 10-yard shuffle to the right	15 sec
• Sprint 8 yards	15 sec
• 10-yard shuffle to the left	40 sec
• Sprint 24 yards	15 sec
• 1–2 steps upfield and take on a trap block from the right	15 sec
• Sprint 10 yards	15 sec
• 1–2 steps upfield and take on a trap block from the left	40 sec

• Sprint 10 yards	15 sec
• Sprint 3 yards, turn left, and sprint 20 yards	15 sec
• Sprint 10 yards	15 sec
• Sprint 3 yards, turn right, and sprint 20 yards	40 sec
• Sprint 10 yards	15 sec
• Sprint 5 yards, spin left, and sprint 5 yards	15 sec
• Sprint 40 yards	15 sec
• Sprint 5 yards, spin right, and sprint 5 yards	40 sec
• Sprint 8 yards	15 sec
• Hoop right	15 sec
• Sprint 24 yards	15 sec
• Hoop left	9 min

Outside Linebackers	**Rest**
• Sprint 15 yards	15 sec
• Exit 45 degrees to the right 10 yards and sprint back to the LOS	15 sec
• Sprint 8 yards	15 sec
• Exit 45 degrees to the left 10 yards, and sprint back to the LOS	40 sec
• Sprint 11 yards	15 sec
• Exit 45 degrees to the right and sprint 25 yards	15 sec
• Sprint 8 yards	15 sec
• Exit 45 degrees to the left and sprint 25 yards	40 sec
• Sprint 10 yards	15 sec
• Backpedal 10 yards, sprint back to the LOS, and exit at 45 degrees	15 sec
• Sprint 25 yards	15 sec
• Backpedal 10 yards, sprint back to the LOS, and exit at 45 degrees	40 sec
• Sprint 8 yards	15 sec
• Backpedal 10 yards, turn, and look over the opposite shoulder	15 sec
• Sprint 30 yards	15 sec
• Backpedal 10 yards, turn, and look over the opposite shoulder	40 sec
• Sprint 8 yards	15 sec
• Lateral shuffle 10 yards and sprint at a 45-degree angle left 5 yards	15 sec
• Sprint 40 yards	15 sec
• Lateral shuffle 10 yards and sprint at a 45-degree angle right 5 yards	9 min

Inside Linebackers	**Rest**
• Sprint 15 yards	15 sec
• Backpedal 5 yards, gather, and explode to the cone	15 sec
• Sprint 8 yards	15 sec
• Backpedal 3 yards and, on command, open to the right. Alternate the direction of the shuffle. Do 3 turns and stay on line for 12 yards.	40 sec
• Sprint 11 yards	15 sec

- Backpedal 3 yards and, on command, open to the right or left. Alternate the direction of the crossover/run. Do 3 turns and stay on line for 12 yards.   15 sec
- Sprint 8 yards   15 sec
- Crossover and work back with width and depth for 5 yards, and then flip your hips and gain ground for 5 yards   40 sec
- Sprint 10 yards   15 sec
- Shuffle and work back with width and depth for 5 yards, and then flip your hips and gain ground for 5 yards   15 sec
- Sprint 25 yards   15 sec
- Backpedal and, on command, break back to the ball at a 45-degree angle   40 sec
- Sprint 8 yards   15 sec
- Backpedal 5 yards, gather, and explode to the cone   15 sec
- Sprint 30 yards   15 sec
- Backpedal 3 yards and, on command, open to the right. Alternate the direction of the shuffle. Do 3 turns and stay on line for 12 yards.   40 sec
- Sprint 8 yards   15 sec
- Backpedal 3 yards and, on command, open to the right or left. Alternate the direction of the crossover/run. Do 3 turns and stay on line for 12 yards.   15 sec
- Sprint 40 yards   15 sec
- Crossover and work back with width and depth for 5 yards, and then flip your hips and gain ground for 5 yards   9 min

Dates: June 27–July 3

Position: Fullbacks

Wednesday—Perform a 300-yard shuttle run, using 25-yard intervals (2 reps; pace: 62 seconds; rest: 5 minutes)

Saturday (2 reps; complete the workout with 100 percent intensity)

	Rest
• Sprint 13 yards	15 sec
• Take play #1 steps and accelerate 15 yards downfield	15 sec
• Sprint 8 yards	15 sec
• Take play #2 steps and accelerate 15 yards downfield	40 sec
• Sprint 40 yards	15 sec
• Take play #3 steps and accelerate 15 yards downfield	15 sec
• Sprint 25 yards	15 sec
• Take play #4 steps, attack space, and accelerate 15 yards downfield	40 sec
• Sprint 25 yards	15 sec
• Take play #5 steps and accelerate 15 yards downfield	15 sec

• Sprint 25 yards	15 sec
• Take play #6 steps and accelerate 15 yards downfield	40 sec
• Sprint 25 yards	15 sec
• Take play #7 steps and accelerate 15 yards downfield	15 sec
• Sprint 25 yards	15 sec
• Take play #8 steps, attack space, and accelerate 15 yards downfield	40 sec
• Sprint 40 yards	15 sec
• Take play #9 steps and accelerate 15 yards downfield	15 sec
• Sprint 15 yards	15 sec
• Take play #10 steps and accelerate 15 yards downfield	10 min

Dates: June 13–June 19

Position: Offensive Linemen (OL)/Tight Ends (TE)

Wednesday—Perform a 300-yard shuttle run, using 25-yard intervals (2 reps; pace: OL 64 seconds, TE 61 seconds; rest: 5 minutes)

Saturday (2 reps; complete the workout with 100 percent intensity)

Offensive Linemen	**Rest**
• Sprint 8 yards	15 sec
• Pop-release right 3 steps and sprint 10 yards	15 sec
• Sprint 6 yards	15 sec
• Pop-release left 3 steps and sprint 10 yards	40 sec
• Sprint 7 yards	15 sec
• Over-and-up step right and sprint upfield 10 yards	15 sec
• Sprint 20 yards	15 sec
• Over-and-up step left and sprint upfield 10 yards	40 sec
• Sprint 6 yards	15 sec
• Drop back right and sprint upfield 10 yards	15 sec
• Sprint 7 yards	15 sec
• Drop back left and sprint upfield 10 yards	40 sec
• Sprint 8 yards	15 sec
• Pull right 5 yards and sprint upfield 10 yards	15 sec
• Sprint 20 yards	15 sec
• Pull left 5 yards and sprint upfield 10 yards	40 sec
• Sprint 8 yards	15 sec
• Bear crawl right 5 yards and sprint upfield 10 yards	15 sec
• Sprint 6 yards	15 sec
• Bear crawl left 5 yards and sprint upfield 10 yards	10 min

Tight Ends	**Rest**
• Sprint 6 yards	15 sec

- Pop-release right 3 steps and sprint 10 yards — 15 sec
- Sprint 40 yards — 15 sec
- Pop release left 3 steps and sprint 10 yards — 40 sec
- Sprint 7 yards — 15 sec
- Over-and-up step right and sprint upfield 10 yards — 15 sec
- Sprint 15 yards — 15 sec
- Over-and-up step left and sprint upfield 10 yards — 40 sec
- Sprint 10 yards — 15 sec
- Drop back right and sprint upfield 10 yards — 15 sec
- Sprint 18 yards — 15 sec
- Drop back left and sprint upfield 10 yards — 40 sec
- Sprint 8 yards — 15 sec
- Search 12 to 10 two-linebacker scheme — 15 sec
- Sprint 20 yards — 15 sec
- Search 12 to 10 three-linebacker scheme — 40 sec
- Sprint 40 yards — 15 sec
- Flag — 15 sec
- Sprint 10 yards — 15 sec
- Post — 10 min

Dates: June 20–June 26

Position: Defensive Linemen/Linebackers

Wednesday—Perform a 300-yard shuttle run, using 25-yard intervals (2 reps; pace: 60 seconds; rest: 4:50)

Saturday (2 reps; complete the workout with 100 percent intensity)

	Rest
Sprint 13 yards	15 sec
Take inside-veer steps to the right and accelerate 15 yards downfield	15 sec
Sprint 8 yards	15 sec
Take trap steps to the right and accelerate 15 yards downfield	40 sec
Sprint 40 yards	15 sec
Take midline steps to the right and accelerate 15 yards downfield	15 sec
Sprint 25 yards	15 sec
Take play-action steps to the right, attack space, and accelerate 15 yards downfield	40 sec
Sprint 25 yards	15 sec
Take inside-veer steps to the left and accelerate 15 yards downfield	15 sec
Sprint 25 yards	15 sec
Take trap steps to the left and accelerate 15 yards downfield	40 sec
Sprint 25 yards	15 sec

• Take midline steps to the left and accelerate 15 yards downfield	15 sec
• Sprint 25 yards	15 sec
• Take play-action steps to the left, attack space, and accelerate 15 yards downfield	40 sec
• Sprint 40 yards	15 sec
• Take inside-veer steps to the right and accelerate 15 yards downfield	15 sec
• Sprint 15 yards	15 sec
• Take inside-veer steps to the left and accelerate 15 yards downfield	9 min

Dates: July 4–July 10

Position: Offensive Linemen (OL)/Tight Ends (TE)

Wednesday—Perform a 300-yard shuttle run, using 25-yard intervals (3 reps; pace: OL 63 seconds, TE 60 seconds; rest: OL 5 minutes, TE 4:45)

Saturday (2 reps; complete the workout with 100 percent intensity)

Offensive Linemen	**Rest**
• Sprint 8 yards	15 sec
• Pop-release right 3 steps and sprint 10 yards	15 sec
• Sprint 6 yards	15 sec
• Pop-release left 3 steps and sprint 10 yards	40 sec
• Sprint 7 yards	15 sec
• Over-and-up step right and sprint upfield 10 yards	15 sec
• Sprint 20 yards	15 sec
• Over-and-up step left and sprint upfield 10 yards	40 sec
• Sprint 6 yards	15 sec
• Drop back right and sprint upfield 10 yards	15 sec
• Sprint 7 yards	15 sec
• Drop back left and sprint upfield 10 yards	40 sec
• Sprint 8 yards	15 sec
• Pull right 5 yards an sprint upfield 10 yards	15 sec
• Sprint 20 yards	15 sec
• Pull left 5 yards and sprint upfield 10 yards	40 sec
• Sprint 8 yards	15 sec
• Bear crawl right 5 yards and sprint upfield 10 yards	15 sec
• Sprint 6 yards	15 sec
• Bear crawl left 5 yards and sprint upfield 10 yards	8 min

Tight Ends	**Rest**
• Sprint 6 yards	15 sec
• Pop-release right 3 steps and sprint 10 yards	15 sec
• Sprint 40 yards	15 sec

- Pop-release left 3 steps and sprint 10 yards | 40 sec
- Sprint 7 yards | 15 sec
- Over-and-up step right and sprint upfield 10 yards | 15 sec
- Sprint 15 yards | 15 sec
- Over-and-up step left and sprint upfield 10 yards | 40 sec
- Sprint 10 yards | 15 sec
- Drop back right and sprint upfield 10 yards | 15 sec
- Sprint 18 yards | 15 sec
- Drop back left and sprint upfield 10 yards | 40 sec
- Sprint 8 yards | 15 sec
- Search 12 to 10 two-linebacker scheme | 15 sec
- Sprint 20 yards | 15 sec
- Search 12 to 10 three-linebacker scheme | 40 sec
- Sprint 40 yards | 15 sec
- Flag | 15 sec
- Sprint 10 yards | 15 sec
- Post | 8 min

Dates: July 11–July 17

Position: Defensive Linemen (DL)/Linebackers (LB)

Wednesday—Perform a 300-yard shuttle run, using 25-yard intervals (3 reps; pace: DL 60 seconds, LB 59 seconds; rest: DL 5 minutes, LB 4:45)

Saturday (4 reps; complete the workout with 100 percent intensity)

Defensive Linemen	Rest
• Sprint 8 yards	15 sec
• 10-yard shuffle to the right	15 sec
• Sprint 8 yards	15 sec
• 10-yard shuffle to the left	40 sec
• Sprint 24 yards	15 sec
• 1–2 steps upfield and take on a trap block from the right	15 sec
• Sprint 10 yards	15 sec
• 1–2 steps upfield and take on a trap block from the right	40 sec
• Sprint 10 yards	15 sec
• Sprint 3 yards, turn left, and sprint 20 yards	15 sec
• Sprint 10 yards	15 sec
• Sprint 3 yards, turn right, and sprint 20 yards	40 sec
• Sprint 10 yards	15 sec
• Sprint 5 yards, spin left, and sprint 5 yards	15 sec
• Sprint 40 yards	15 sec
• Sprint 5 yards, spin right, and sprint 5 yards	40 sec

• Sprint 8 yards	15 sec
• Hoop right	15 sec
• Sprint 24 yards	15 sec
• Hoop left	8 min

Outside Linebackers — Rest

• Sprint 15 yards	15 sec
• Exit 45 degrees to the right 10 yards, and sprint back to the LOS	15 sec
• Sprint 8 yards	15 sec
• Exit 45 degrees to the left 10 yards, and sprint back to the LOS	40 sec
• Sprint 11 yards	15 sec
• Exit 45 degrees to the right and sprint 25 yards	15 sec
• Sprint 8 yards	15 sec
• Exit 45 degrees to the left and sprint 25 yards	40 sec
• Sprint 10 yards	15 sec
• Backpedal 10 yards, sprint back to the LOS, exit at 45 degrees	15 sec
• Sprint 25 yards	15 sec
• Backpedal 10 yards, sprint back to the LOS, exit at 45 degrees	40 sec
• Sprint 8 yards	15 sec
• Backpedal 10 yards, turn, and look over the opposite shoulder	15 sec
• Sprint 30 yards	15 sec
• Backpedal 10 yards, turn, and look over the opposite shoulder	40 sec
• Sprint 8 yards	15 sec
• Lateral shuffle 10 yards and sprint at a 45-degree angle left 5 yards	15 sec
• Sprint 40 yards	15 sec
• Lateral shuffle 10 yards and sprint at a 45-degree angle right 5 yards	8 min

Inside Linebackers — Rest

• Sprint 15 yards	15 sec
• Backpedal 5 yards, gather, and explode to the cone	15 sec
• Sprint 8 yards	15 sec
• Backpedal 3 yards and, on command, open to the right. Alternate the direction of the shuffle. Do 3 turns and stay on line for 12 yards.	40 sec
• Sprint 11 yards	15 sec
• Backpedal 3 yards and, on command, open to the right or left. Alternate the direction of the crossover/run. Do 3 turns and stay on line for 12 yards.	15 sec
• Sprint 8 yards	15 sec
• Crossover and work back with width and depth for 5 yards, and then flip your hips and gain ground for 5 yards	40 sec
• Sprint 10 yards	15 sec
• Shuffle and work back with width and depth for 5 yards, and then flip your hips and gain ground for 5 yards	15 sec
• Sprint 25 yards	15 sec

- Backpedal and, on command, break back to the ball at a 45-degree
  angle   40 sec
- Sprint 8 yards   15 sec
- Backpedal 5 yards, gather, and explode to the cone   15 sec
- Sprint 30 yards   15 sec
- Backpedal 3 yards and, on command, open to the right. Alternate the
  direction of the shuffle. Do 3 turns and stay on line for 12 yards. 40 sec
- Sprint 8 yards   15 sec
- Backpedal 3 yards and, on command, open to the right or left.
  Alternate the direction of the crossover/run. Do 3 turns and stay on line
  for 12 yards.   15 sec
- Sprint 40 yards   15 sec
- Crossover and work back with width and depth for 5 yards, and then
  flip your hips and gain ground for 5 yards   8 min

Dates: July 18–July 31

Position: Fullbacks

Wednesday—Perform a 300-yard shuttle run, using 25-yard intervals (3 reps; pace: 59 seconds; rest: 4:45)

Saturday (2 reps; complete the workout with 100 percent intensity)

	Rest
- Sprint 13 yards	15 sec
- Take play #1 steps and accelerate 15 yards downfield	15 sec
- Sprint 8 yards	15 sec
- Take play #2 steps and accelerate 15 yards downfield	40 sec
- Sprint 40 yards	15 sec
- Take play #3 steps and accelerate 15 yards downfield	15 sec
- Sprint 25 yards	15 sec
- Take play #4 steps, attack space, and accelerate 15 yards downfield	40 sec
- Sprint 25 yards	15 sec
- Take play #5 steps and accelerate 15 yards downfield	15 sec
- Sprint 25 yards	15 sec
- Take play #6 steps and accelerate 15 yards downfield	40 sec
- Sprint 25 yards	15 sec
- Take play #7 steps and accelerate 15 yards downfield	15 sec
- Sprint 25 yards	15 sec
- Take play #8 steps, attack space, and accelerate 15 yards downfield	40 sec
- Sprint 40 yards	15 sec
- Take play #9 steps and accelerate 15 yards downfield	15 sec
- Sprint 15 yards	15 sec
- Take play #10 steps and accelerate 15 yards downfield	7 mi

About the Author

Allen Hedrick, M.A., CSCS*D, Coach Practitioner, is the head strength and conditioning coach at the United States Air Force Academy, a position he has held since 1998. Among the areas for which he has responsibility are program design and supervision of all aspects of the strength, plyometric, and speed training for football and volleyball, while also overseeing the entire strength and conditioning program at the Academy. Prior to assuming his present position, he served as an assistant strength and conditioning coach at USAF for three years. Before that, he was the strength and conditioning coordinator at the U.S. Olympic Training Center for three years. A graduate of California State University, Fresno, Hedrick is a prolific author, a much sought-after clinician, and a featured speaker on a number of well-received instructional videos. In 2003, he was named the NSCA's College Strength and Conditioning Professional of the Year.